CW00336756

London Transport
Since 1963

London
Transport
Since 1963

Michael H. C. Baker

IAN ALLAN *Publishing*

First published 1997

ISBN 0 7110 2481 2

Published by Ian Allan Publishing

an imprint of Ian Allan Ltd,
Terminal House, Station Approach,
Shepperton, Surrey TW17 8AS.
Printed by Ian Allan Printing Ltd,
Coombelands House, Coombelands
Lane, Addlestone, Surrey KT15 1HY.

Front cover: RM2038 working
route 137. *Author*

Back cover, top: Ruislip depot.
Brian Morrison

Back cover, bottom: Eastbound
1992 stock at East Acton.
John Glover

Contents

Foreword

Within these pages we record the types, the changes, the liveries, the contractions and expansions, some of the people and a few personal reminiscences of the last 30 years of London Transport. With its companion volume *London Transport 1933–1962* it completes the 60-year old history of the largest urban transport undertaking in the world.

1963

For the first time since the turn of the century a new year began in London with no electrically powered passenger vehicles on the streets – unless one counted the odd milk boy getting a lift on his float. Would they ever return? Read on. A change which few members of the public noticed was the disappearance of the London Transport Executive and its replacement by the London Transport Board (LTB). If you looked closely, the legal lettering on the lower nearside panels of buses altered but nothing much else on the surface did.

If the weather had been seasonal 12 months earlier, it was even more so at the beginning of 1963. Snow was heavy enough in London but out on the North Downs and elsewhere in the Country Area roads were blocked and buses were abandoned. I watched 403s struggling up Sanderstead Hill and they could get no further south than Chelsham. Dunton Green garage was snowbound, its fleet immobile, as was Crawley. To the north, Hertford and Stevenage garages were also out of action. For weeks there was no sign of a thaw and snow remained piled by the roadsides into March. It is hard to imagine such conditions in the London area in the 1990s.

Apart from the weather, on the whole 1963 was a less dramatic year than many. Routemasters continued to be delivered, replacing RTs and RTLs, although there were still so many of the former, and the onslaught on the latter seemed to have eased, so that, other than in central London where they were significant, the changes were not particularly noticeable.

The 'prewar' RTs, withdrawn from passenger service in 1957, had seemed to be a permanent fixture

Below:
The very last 'Prewar' RT – RT79 at Dunton Green garage shortly before withdrawal. All pictures by the author or from the Ian Allan Library unless credited otherwise

in the trainer fleet, so long had they served in this role, but with so many postwar RTs and RTLs now surplus their time had come and the last, green RT79, was delicensed, appropriately at a Country Area garage, Dunton Green, on 13 February.

Another standard class to have its ranks reduced was the RF. One, RF464, was burnt out at Fulwell garage while 10 of the one-time private hire coaches, 16-25, converted to Green Line use, were sold. The GS class, already reduced in numbers, also began to find new owners. GS3 and GS4 were pioneers in a process which would become commonplace in future decades, that of remaining within LT territory with their new owners. They went to Tillingbourne Valley, which operated, jointly with LT, route 448 from Guildford to Peaslake and they actually found themselves working alongside GSs from Guildford garage.

Croydon had long been promised a bus station and at last, in July, it opened at West Croydon, alongside the back end of the railway station and on the site where the route 630 trolleybuses used to turn. It was a handy spot for photographers, having plenty of fresh air and daylight, but by the same token was not over-endowed with creature comforts for the customers, who were, after all, the first priority. It would be several decades before the situation improved. Nearly 1,000 buses used it each Monday to Friday.

Returning to central London a curious contrivance, something like a giant molehill, appeared at Oxford Circus over the August Bank Holiday. London's newest tube railway, the Victoria line, of which more anon, passed under it and to enable the new interchange station to be constructed the road had to be removed and an umbrella of steel girders erected in its place. This hump was tarmacked over and was ready for traffic within three days, although only southbound and westbound vehicles were allowed to use it.

Production of Routemasters continued throughout the year. A small, but pleasing, visual variation which took place in 1963 was the fitting of the traditional AEC triangle to the radiator, both to new buses and to many earlier ones as well. Once conversion to Routemasters of route 16 was completed early in January, the 36A and 36B, which kept the 16 company from Victoria, along Park Lane and up the Edgware Road as far as Praed Street, followed. Next came route 9, then 43, then 63, followed by the suburban route 85 and 85A, then back to central London for the 14. Until now the 8ft wide RTWs had been, to all intents and purposes, unaffected but route 14, worked by Putney garage, had been one of their strongholds – they had taken it over from the 'prewar' 2RTs. Most of the RTWs displaced went to Brixton garage, joining some newly arrived RTLs, but four were downgraded to learners. Many more RTWs went into the training fleet when RMs moved on to that interesting route, the 24, which was to see so many different, and often unusual, types in the years to come. The last conversion of all was route 7 in December, when Middle Row garage began to move out its RTLs.

The Leylands were generally regarded with less favour than the AECs both by drivers because of the heavier steering and by the engineers on account of problems with engine changes; because of this the RTs would outlive both RTLs and RTWs in passenger service in London by some 11 years.

In November a new crossing of the Thames, much nearer the sea than any other, opened in November when the Dartford Tunnel came into use. A new Country Area route, 300, made use of it, running between Grays and Dartford; an existing Green Line route was extended through it, while five curious looking Strachan-bodied, Thames Trader double-deckers operated a service for cyclists and pedestrians. They were owned by the Tunnel Authority and crewed by LT. None of the services were very well patronised and all have long since gone.

Apart from the Green Line Routemasters no RMs had yet appeared in the Country Area. However withdrawal of green-liveried roof-box RTs began in the summer and to replace them red RTs were repainted and overhauled. Various refinements had been fitted to RTs over the years, notably trafficators and heaters, although the latter only to Country Area vehicles, the thinking being presumably that the rural parts were colder than the suburban and central London ones. There were several flaws in this, not the least being that many Country Area routes were actually far more suburban than rural in character. Tacit recognition of this was given in 1963 with the announcement that, with the completion of the programme in the Country Area – apart from the roof-box RTs scheduled for early withdrawal – red RTs with an expected lifespan of eight or more years would also have heaters. No RTLs or RTWs ever had them. A Chelsham conductor told me that he thought an RT fitted with heaters was the acme of double-deck bus comfort and in all respects superior to an RM; he was not alone in holding this opinion.

Below:
RT1079 battles through the snow in Oxford Street.

1964

1964 saw the decline in the RT family fleet continue.
One of the sub-groups which disappeared was the
Country Area roof-box RT, the last of which ended its
passenger duties 10 days into 1964. This distinctive
and virtually unique feature would last some time
longer in the Central Area and an interesting variation
appeared when RTLs began to appear from overhaul
with this type of body. Previously the prototype
RTL501 had been unique in this respect but 21 RTLs
were fitted with roof-box bodies in 1964. The thinking
behind this was that both the RTL and this type of
body had not long to go in LT ownership and so they
might as well be paired. In March the very last
'prewar' RTs still owned by LT, Nos 88 and 118,
were sold and broken up by Cohen's.

One of our local garages, Carshalton, best known as
home of route 654 trolleybuses, went out of business
at the end of January, most of its RTs moving to the
former Daimler strongholds of Sutton and Merton.
One route linking Croydon with central London no
longer did so after the end of January when route 133
was cut back from South Croydon garage to Thornton
Heath high street. This was part of a trend becoming
common with many of the longer LT trunk routes.
Increasing congestion, chiefly caused by private cars,
meant the longer a route the greater the opportunity
for delays, and so they were gradually being broken
into more manageable, shorter sections. Thus new
route 133A was inaugurated between South Croydon
and Kennington, being extended at peak times to
Victoria Embankment.

Another local event which typified what was
happening throughout the system was the appearance
of RTWs at the top of our road in Thornton Heath.
Displaced from their familiar haunts by Routemasters
they had been sent to Brixton to work the tram
replacement route 109. Apart from the brand-new
batch which worked out of Bromley for a short time
on route 119, this was the first, and last, time RTWs
were seen regularly in Croydon, and Purley was the
furthest south they were ever to reach.

It would be tedious to list all the routes which were
taken over by Routemasters as the year progressed but
some are certainly worth recording. In April Upton
Park garage began to receive the type for the 15; 31
years later Upton Park still operates Routemasters, of

Above:
Country Area roof-box RT992 and RT3617 at Kingston.

several varieties, on the 15. Later they took up work
on the 3 and the 137, both of which routes still see
regular Routemaster workings.

No London bus type has ever remained completely
standard and inevitably there were changes, some
minor, some more radical, to the Routemaster as its
numbers grew. RM1923 appeared with an illuminated
advert on its offside and was sent to Putney to work
route 30. Many more such RMs appeared in 1964.
Naturally enough this group of buses was restricted to
routes which worked through central London thus
ensuring the maximum exposure and, it was hoped,
making the exercise a profitable one.

Many people had wondered for some years what
would happen when the last Y prefix registrations –
there would be no 'Zs' – were used up. 1963 proved
to be the crunch year and all was revealed when
vehicles began to appear with an 'A' suffix. LT had
still plenty of CLTs and DYEs to use up and it wasn't
until the spring of 1964 that the first suffixes appeared
on Routemasters with Upton Park's new buses
starting with RM1866, ALD 866B. RM2000 arrived
in September and was given the registration ALM
200B while the 'B' series ended on 31 December with
RM2105, ALM 105B.

In the 1960s unemployment was virtually unknown,
certainly in the London area, and the unsocial hours

and declining pay in comparison to other jobs of busmen meant staff shortages. Recruiting was actively carried out in the Caribbean and this helped but did not totally overcome the problem. Private hire and tours were let go to other operators and thus the RFW coaches, which had spent their entire careers in this employment, were all taken out of service and sold.

Tackling the problem from another angle, and also cutting costs, one-man operation (OMO) at last began in the Central Area. The date was 18 November and was one of great significance: getting rid of the conductor was seen as the panacea for the

ills of the bus industry and would become virtually universal outside the capital. Central London, late to embrace it, would by the 1990s be the only part of the kingdom where two-person buses were still to be seen in large numbers; where there were others these would almost always be operated by ex-LT Routemasters.

It is worth recording the routes which became one-man (women drivers had not yet arrived on the scene) operated. They were all worked by RFs: three from Kingston garage, the 201, 206, and 216, and the 250 worked by Hornchurch.

Left:
RM2179 with illuminated offside advertisement panel passing Battersea Park station whilst working the 137.

Below left:
RF369 in Kingston bus station.

Right:
Godstone RT986 working route 410.

Below:
The Shuttle from Acton Town at South Acton. *Dr H. Zinram*

By the end of 1964 the fleet had declined by some 250 vehicles, most of those withdrawn being RTs and RTLs, although some RFs, GSs, RLHs (the first two) all but two of the 15 RFWs and one TD (leaving just one in the fleet) had also been sold. What was probably the best known London lowbridge route, the 410, was diverted to avoid the reason for its existence in November; RTs replaced the RLHs and it was a lowbridge route no longer. As someone who a little later went to live in Oxted, I could only wonder why the diversion hadn't been made decades earlier and thus the inconvenience of producing several one-off designs avoided.

On the Underground the section of District Line between Acton Town and Hounslow West closed, it being covered by the Piccadilly Line.

The London bus (and tram, train and trolleybus) had always had a considerable following amongst small boys, big boys and grown men, although, sadly, rather less so with the female sex. The Ian Allan *abcs* and associated publications beginning in the 1940s had, for the first time, provided really comprehensive information and pictures and in 1964 another dimension was added to the steadily growing hobby observing and recording in the minutest detail London's vast public transport network when the London Omnibus Traction Society (LOTS) was founded.

A year earlier enthusiasts had hardly been able to contain themselves when, at long last after years of illicit sneaking into Reigate garage, the collection of preserved London vehicles had gone on display at the Museum of British Transport in Clapham, alongside *Mallard*, carriages from the royal train, a Brighton trolleybus and many other treasures, large and small. The premises had been a bus garage, a relatively new one built on the site of Clapham tram depot. It was not destined to be permanent and the LT section would eventually be separated from the railway exhibits which would go to York, but it was a wonderful display.

1965

The dawn of what we might call the modern age of bus travel in London, which had peeped over the horizon in a cold late autumn morning in 1964 when OMO began on four red single-deck routes, tiptoed a little further into the daylight on 15 September. Eight rear-engined Daimler Fleetline double-deckers with Park Royal bodies began work from East Grinstead garage. This was, admittedly, about as far as you could get from central London and still come across a LT bus – Southdown and Maidstone & District (M&D) also had garages in the town – but it was the start for all that, and in the autumn the rear-engined bus finally arrived in central London.

LT had already announced plans for trials of a new generation of double and single-deckers and on

7 November the XA class – which would eventually number 50 – entered service from Chalk Farm garage on route 24 from Hampstead Heath to Pimlico. The X stood for experimental, the A stood for Atlantean; if you were prepared to stand for these monsters you were prepared to stand for anything, ho, ho! A bit harsh perhaps, but they were crude vehicles, with standard provincial Park Royal bodies, not very well proportioned externally, and internally very basic, far below the standards which the RT and RM provided. They had sliding vents, unlike the more sophisticated winding windows hitherto standard, and they also introduced a new livery variation in that the pale cream band became pale grey – which sometimes was quite noticeable, and sometimes wasn't. There was no reason why the first generation of rear-engined double-deckers had to be ugly – they just were. The Atlantean was not very reliable either, although this may partly have been because LT engineers found it so unfamiliar. Having front-entrance power-operated doors Londoners could no longer hop on and off whenever they felt like it and this, too, contributed to their unpopularity. For all that the Routemaster suddenly looked rather old-fashioned beside them; the RT more so.

However the RM was still in full production, or rather the RML for the last of the shorter vehicles was delivered in May. The next batch consisted of 43 coaches, similar to the RMCs, but seating an extra row of passengers on each deck, 65 in all. The front

Above left:
XF8 newly in service working out of East Grinstead (EG) garage on route 424.

Above:
XA10 in Trafalgar Square following an RM on route 15 with an RTW on the 11 alongside.

Below:
RTLs from Victoria (GM) could be seen working on route 11 until November 1965. Newly overhauled RTL1519 is seen inside its home garage.

end, still with twin headlights, was slightly modified, as was the route indicator, while the livery was a little different. All of this produced what many considered the most handsome of all the Routemaster variations. Numbered RCL2218-2260 (CUV 218C-260C), they were sent to Romford, Grays and Hertford.

More new coaches arrived in the Green Line fleet at the end of the year. As handsome as the RCLs, these were 14 AEC Reliance single-deckers with Willowbrook bodies. These were to the BET pattern, found in great numbers at that time in such fleets as Southdown, M&D and East Kent and wore a striking new livery of pale grey with a green waist band. Measuring 36ft long and 8ft 2.5in wide, they were fitted for the first time in LT history with proper coach seats. They went to Windsor and Dunton Green garages to operate route 705.

Immediately following the RCLs, delivery of red-liveried RMLs commenced. They were virtually

identical to the pioneer batch of 1961, RML880-903. Starting with RML2261 they had CUV xxxC registrations, like the RCLs and the majority of the XAs, and some were put to work in direct comparison with the latter. The RML achieved a fuel consumption of 7.8mpg, making it a most economical bus, and over a mile a gallon better than the heavier XA; fleet-wide this amounted to a considerable saving for LT.

Comparison between front and rear-engined buses was not immediately possible as the XAs were not yet ready so some new RMLs were sent, somewhat surprisingly, to the Country Area at Godstone. Brand new red RTs had appeared in the Country Area and new green ones in central London but until now the only Routemasters seen in the outer reaches of Chiswick's empire had been Green Line ones. It was intended that the 409, 410 and 411 routes should all go over to RML operations so they were sent to East Grinstead, Godstone and Reigate garages too. Yet another first for the Croydon area! Their stay was short for green RMLs were also being delivered and soon there were enough to allow the red ones to return to the Central Area where they went to Tottenham to work the 76 alongside other newly delivered members of the class, while XAs took up work from Chalk Farm on the 24. More red RMLs went to Stamford Hill for the 67. Either directly or indirectly they replaced many RTWs and this class was now well on the way out.

Meanwhile more new green RMLs arrived at Northfleet where their principal duties were on route 480. A minor, but noticeable, variation, which would become standard, on the constantly fascinating topic of destination blinds first appeared at Godstone when the rear via box was given over to nothing but a large route number.

By the end of 1965 only 144 RTWs were scheduled for operation Monday to Friday. Interestingly they still clung on to route 11, London's most famous route. Sixteen years earlier I had my last glimpse of a Bluebird LT also at work on the 11. However there the comparison ends, for although the LTs, having exceeded their intended lifespan and suffered the neglect of the war years, really were worn out, while to the passenger the RTWs seemed almost as good as new. In fact they were getting on for 16 years old and although many found new owners, they were never very popular with crews being the heaviest of all the RT variants to steer. After a shift on route 11 one certainly knew one had done a day's work.

The RTL fleet declined by over a hundred during 1965, although proportionally this was much less than their fatter Leyland brothers, while there was actually an increase in scheduled RT numbers. The very last TD, No 118, had been sold.

A change, which could have had a huge effect on the public transport scene in London if it had been allowed, took place in April 1965 when the Greater London Council (GLC) came into being. It planned, as we shall see, to make London a more egalitarian place to live and visit, where subsidised public transport would be so cheap and convenient that there would be little need for the private car. Entrenched vested interests and a pretty peculiar reading of the word freedom eventually won the day – but it was a brave try.

One attempt, or rather many on the same theme, tried throughout the year to improve traffic flow was the introduction of one way schemes, the most grandiose being that around Victoria. One traditional feature no longer encountered was the meeting of the many Green Line services on Eccleston Bridge above the long extended platforms of Victoria station, for this now became one way. However Victoria remained, and indeed remains, very much Green Line territory.

1966

Above:
XMS4 in Park Lane. *IAL*

Below:
XMS2 in later years working for London Country from Leatherhead garage.

On 31 July 1966 Bobby Moore climbed to the royal box at Wembley Stadium to collect the World Cup . If that was the high point of English football, a few weeks later an announcement heralded an equally momentous event in LT's history. The one-man bus would become standard. Elsewhere rear and underfloor engines enabling the entrance to be beside the driver at the front of the bus were becoming almost universal, facilitating the demise of the conductor, which reduced costs. This was the primary objective of nearly all bus companies, desperate to fight the motor car which was taking away their passengers throughout England, Wales and Scotland, whether out in the villages and the country towns or in the cities and conurbations.

High capacity single-deckers were already on order and the first of these arrived in February. They were AEC Merlins with rear engines and a Strachan body which seated 25 with standing room for no less than 48. Londoners weren't at all used to this, although commuters in many other European cities were. Designated the XMS they began work on the first Red Arrow service, route 500 Victoria-Marble Arch, on 18 April. They stopped only at Hyde Park Corner during the rush hours, and ran for shoppers outside these periods. The journey cost 4d instead of 6d on the ordinary routes; it was certainly faster and was rather popular, although not because of the automatic ticket machines, which proved very unreliable.

There were six of these XMSs. Nine similar XMBs in green livery with 46 seats were also delivered but only one actually worked in the Country Area. The

Right:
Brixton (BN) was the last garage to operate RTWs. One stands here beside an RT at Thornton Heath.

Below:
RMF1254 after being sold to Northern General at Newcastle in 1978.

rest were converted to XMS standard and repainted red.

Meanwhile the passenger carrying days of the RTW were drawing to an end. In February they at last relinquished their hold on route 11; in April they disappeared from the 22, and in May from the 95 and 109. The very last, RTW467, ran in to Brixton garage

off the 95 at 00.30 on 15 May. For a while, as with the 'prewar' RTs with which they seemed to have an affinity working as they did from the same garages, they continued in learner service.

No amount of one way schemes, fine new Routemasters, or avant garde rear-engined double-deckers and high capacity single-deckers could defeat

the private car and yet more service cuts in both May and June saw many RTLs delicensed.

Two more variations on the Routemaster theme appeared in 1966. In October the first of 65 front-entrance buses for BEA took up work. They replaced the one and a half deck RFs and were basically to the design of the RMF, but shorter so they could legally tow luggage trailers. RMF1254 left London in November. It was sold to Northern General which already had a fleet of front entrance RMs. In its four years with LT it never entered ordinary passenger service and was the first Routemaster to be sold by LT. My experience of seeing this bus of pure LT design on ordinary stage carriage work but twice, once in Liverpool and once in Newcastle, can hardly have been unique.

Above:
A group of BEA Routemasters, some repainted into British Airways livery.

Below:
FRM1 at Roundshaw whilst working from Croydon (TC) garage on route 233.

There was another variation on the Routemaster theme, which I saw many times working in the LT area and which was completed in 1966; this was FRM1. One of the great might-have-beens of British bus history, this was a belated attempt by AEC to enter the rear-engined double-deck market. It contained 60 per cent standard Routemaster parts and was unmistakably one of the family. Far handsomer than the XAs and XFs, although perhaps rather staid compared to some later stylish rear-engined body designs, it did not enter passenger service until 1967.

OMO continued to spread and now reached the Green Line network. A new route covering some 70 miles in the far northern reaches was the 724, which ran from High Wycombe by way of Watford, St Albans, Welwyn Garden City, Hertford and Epping to Romford and was worked by OMO RFs from the garages at the extremities of its route. It was a bold venture, very much the northern version of the 725, and very nearly as successful.

Crew-operated operation of RFs had almost come to an end in the Country Area by the end of 1966 and although many of the Green Line vehicles were being refurbished with a two-tone livery, twin headlights and fluorescent lighting, passengers were deserting the Green Line network with considerable enthusiasm, either heading for their cars or the ever-growing electrified British Rail network.

The bus industry has always involved working unsocial hours and on the very last day of 1966 a five-day week was introduced in order to bring about better conditions. Sunday bus operation was declining rapidly; no more were red buses needed to help with the crowds heading for the country and a sign of the times was that there were actually more RMs scheduled for operation in the Central Area on Sundays than RTs, while the number of RTLs at work on that day was now less than 100. Only 261 buses in total worked in the Country Area on Sundays, compared with 893 Monday to Friday. Both the RLH and the GS were well on the way to extinction.

1967

1967 was a less dramatic year than many in that only one new type of bus entered service, and this was destined to remain a one-off. On 26 June FRM1 took up work from Tottenham garage on route 76, working alongside the XAs. It had a forced air ventilation system, which looked a little odd in that there were no opening windows of any description, except beside the driver. No doubt we should have got used to this but the system was not a success. Leaking flywheel oil resulted in FRM1 burning its rear end quite severely in the last day of August, the damage added to by London's brave fire brigade, Matilda style, bashing away at its engine compartment. However a period of convalescence and some nice new opening windows saw it back at work from Tottenham before the year was out.

RMLs continued to come off the production line, but not for much longer. The nine years of standard

Below:
RTLs at Victoria in 1967, alongside an RM on the 16 and an RT on the 38. On the far right is RTL458 while next to it is RTL384, which was one of 23 members of the class fitted with roof-box bodies in 1964.

Left:
RTW28 on learner duty at Morden.

Below:
Modernised Green Line RF66 of St Albans Garage working route 727. *G. Mead*

Bottom:
RF313 was one of the precursors of the modernised RFs; along with others working route 711, it was repainted at the beginning of the 1960s in a lighter shade of green.

Above:
RML2563 of Putney (AF) garage at Isleworth.

RM building exceeded that of the postwar RT by one year, although there had been more than double the number of the earlier bus, to say nothing of the RTL and the RTW. The final Routemaster registration appeared in August, SMK xxxF, with RML2658. However we have not quite reached the end so let us not anticipate.

The other great stalwart of the early postwar years, the RF, still had plenty of life in it and the programme of modernising the Green Line version, mentioned earlier with twin headlights, a new livery with a broad, pale green waistband, and an improved interior, was completed by the spring of 1967 More one-man Green Line RFs went into service in April on the longest Green Line route yet, the 727 operating between Luton and Crawley. The principal feature of the limited stop 727 was that it linked Gatwick, Heathrow and Luton airports, a pointer to the future and to a network of routes which would eventually be hived off to become a separate entity. RFs with extra luggage space were provided. The service proved so popular that later the larger RCs took over. These handsome looking but mechanically unreliable vehicles were not one of LT's better buys. However this was true of a whole generation of single-deckers about to appear on the streets of London and its suburbs and the RCs' contribution to the 727 story was fairly minimal.

RTLs continued to be withdrawn as RMLs continued to be delivered. The last Metro-Cammell members of the class had gone by the end of May and in September the last garage to operate nothing but RTLs – Clapton – received a batch of RTs to begin their replacement. By the end of the year only 216

RTLs were scheduled for operation Monday to Friday, while the Sunday total was down to a paltry 28. Many RTs withdrawn from the Country Area, whether on account of being replaced by RMLs, single-deckers or service cuts, were repainted red and helped bring about the end of their Leyland brothers.

The autumn saw the RMLs enter the 27xx series, and just as the final standard FXT-registered STLs had gone to Hanwell when new, so some of the 27xx RMLs also entered service there. Many also came to Croydon garage from November where they were put to work on the 130 group of routes. Here their extra capacity proved useful for there were always plenty of clients anxious to quit its windy slopes on Monday to Friday mornings though they mostly had to return each evening.

In December details of the revolution which was about to engulf LT were announced. The Country Area would be taken out of LT control and given to the new National Bus Company (NBC). It was ironic that it was a Conservative government which set up the GLC, to whom LT would be handed over, for the GLC under Ken Livingston (Red Ken as the *Evening Standard* liked to call him) became a fierce thorn in the side of Maggie Thatcher, to the extent that she eventually managed to wipe it out – which benefited no-one except 'she who must be obeyed'. If Ken Livingston had been rather more subtle and Margaret Thatcher less vindictive, London might today have a

for the Post Office each year from 1958 to 1963; the former was the last time there had been a delivery on Christmas Day. Bus services had not yet gone the same way but they were headed in that direction and were cut by half compared with 1966.

1968

1968 was one of the most eventful years in LT's history, though no doubt there were some pretty big events in many of our personal lives that year. But I digress. We'll begin with the opening of the Victoria Line. A serious gap in the Underground/tube network was the lack of a direct link between Victoria and Piccadilly, Euston, St Pancras and King's Cross. The Victoria Line was designed to fill this and the government had sanctioned it on 20 August 1962, although plans had existed, in embryo form, since the 1940s. It was quite the most ambitious Underground

better integrated and cheaper public transport network, with fewer motor cars clogging up the works; but such is the vanity of politicians. The Ted Heath government put forward proposals which today sound like pure socialism. Grants of up to 75 per cent would be available for capital investment in facilities such as bus stations and interchanges, and new one-man buses attracted a 25 per cent grant. Further money was available for research, while local authorities could subsidise rural bus services, to which the government would contribute 50 per cent.

With the inexorable advance of the private car and television there was less and less demand for public transport on Christmas Day. The five-day week also complicated the situation. As a student I had worked

Left:
The last Routemaster, RML2760, seen at Trafalgar Square in later years working the X15 from Upton Park (U) garage.

Below:
Red Arrow MBA492.

or tube scheme for decades and the first service trains began to run on 1 September on the northernmost section from Walthamstow Central to Blackhorse Road, Tottenham Hale, Seven Sisters, Finsbury Park and Highbury and Islington. Three months later the section on to King's Cross and St Pancras, Euston and Warren Street opened. The most needed section, on to Victoria, would have to wait until the next year, while the final extension, to Brixton, would not be ready until 1971.

The Victoria Line was revolutionary in a number of respects. In the late 1930s LT had taken industrial design and its associated arts, such as poster design, to new heights but it had seemed to lose its way by the

1950s. The Victoria Line was a reassuring re-affirmation of this fine tradition. Each station was instantly recognisable from its brothers by its own motif, picked out in tiled panels and designed by highly respected artists. Edward Bawden, for instance, provided Highbury and Islington with a high bury, or castle or manor, the original having been destroyed during the Peasants' Revolt, while Crosby, Fletcher and Forbes produced a complex maze, or warren for Warren Street.

Automatic fare collection, now the norm on the Underground system, was installed for the opening of the Victoria Line. Most important of all, the trains were controlled automatically, from a central control

Right:
Country Area Merlins MB89 and MBS434 at Redhill.

room near Euston. This wasn't immediately obvious for there was a driver in the front cab of each train. In reality it would have been more accurate to call him a guard for his chief function was to open and close the doors. When the train was ready to start he merely pressed a button and the automatic control system then took over. He could, in an emergency, over-ride this and he was also in telephone communication with the control room. Fitted with wrap around windscreens, an improvement over the rather bland visages of their predecessors, the 1967 Victoria Line cars originally consisted of 122 driving cars and 122 trailers, others being added later. They had rheostatic brakes, a combined traction/brake controller, powerful headlights and a public address system. For the first

time they carried the legend 'Underground' instead of the hitherto universal 'London Transport'.

As big a milestone was the delivery of the last Routemaster. Only nine were still to come when 1968 opened. All but one went to Croydon garage. The odd one out was the last of all. This, RML2760, together with Croydon's 2754/6, started work on 1 March. No 2760 went to Upton Park. It has been a celebrity all its life, often appearing at rallies and various special events but it still lives at Upton Park and its regular beat, as from its first day in service, is route 15, which now operates between Canning Town and Paddington. 27 years on the same route from the same garage must be some sort of record in the annals of public transport. Two RMLs, which had been on an overseas

Left:
The interior of a Central Area MB.

Below:
The last RTLs were withdrawn from passenger service in 1968 but a few remained a little longer in the training fleet. RTL1223 was one of 18 which had been painted green and sent to work from Hatfield garage in July 1960, lasting less than a year in this role. It stands alongside RT3274 and RT422, the latter by this date nominally the oldest bus in LT passenger service, having been delivered with a body identical to that borne by RT3274, to Leyton garage in September 1947.

tour, entered service a little later, at the end of May, and over the years, as we shall see, other Routemasters have taken up passenger work with LT after various careers elsewhere. But construction had ended.

At this time it was thought that the RM, an outdated design by 1968, might well not last very much longer and that the later ones would be lucky to live out their full lifespan with LT. Unlike the RT family, which had swept away all its predecessors, the RM had certainly not done for the RT, nor even quite the RTL, a few members of which lingered on. Nevertheless front engines, half cabs and open rear platforms were rapidly becoming anachronisms in 1968 and the rear-engined Atlantean and Fleetline were the choice of most bus companies, unless you happened to be a member of the Tilling family, when you were wedded to the front-entrance Lodekka, although not for much longer. But the future is notoriously unpredictable, perhaps fortunately, and the Routemaster has proved to be astonishingly long-lived – and not just in London.

The new era, which – it was confidently assumed – would sweep away RTs, RMs and all such ancient concepts, dawned on 7 September. On that day Red Arrow routes 501 to 507 started operation, along with a complete reshaping of routes in the Walthamstow and Wood Green areas, 22 OMO services in all. The revolutionary buses provided were 36ft long, 8ft 2.5in wide AEC Merlin single-deckers, fitted with MCW bodies. Although the chassis was basically of standard provincial design there were certain modifications. The body was similar to that of the experimental Merlins but rather neater, particularly at the front end. For the first time slide vents were provided in the windows on a standard body for London requirements, a retrograde step in the author's opinion.

There were three variations. The MBA worked the Red Arrow routes. There were 44 of these little beauties. They seated 25, with additional room for 48 standing passengers. You entered at the front; if you didn't have the exact money, 6d to be exact, a machine might give you change, although it might not. You left by centre doors.

The MBS class for use in the suburbs was virtually identical to the Red Arrows, with the same layout and capacity. They also had MCW bodies. The Merlins flooded into London throughout 1968 (though many did not enter service for months). By November they had appeared in green livery in the Country Area, at Reigate, Amersham and High Wycombe.

The third version was the MB which had seats for all its passengers. The Central Area version had doors only at the front and had seats for 50 passengers; the green version retained the centre exit and had 45 seats. One MBA, six MBSs and 13 MBs were licensed early enough in 1968 to receive F suffixes to their registrations; the rest were Gs.

The Merlin was bad news for the RT and the RTL for it was designed to replace these veterans. The new buses were not necessarily any more comfortable but with mounting losses LT had little option but to go over to OMO and the 36ft long single-deckers could equal the RT's capacity. The new Red Arrow services saw an extensive revision of many long-established central London routes, while there were many other changes elsewhere on the network. Buses ceased to run through Rotherhithe Tunnel while MBs took over from RTs on route 108 through the Blackwall Tunnel.

The final RTL routes, the 176 and the 226 worked by Cricklewood, succumbed to MBSs on 29 November; RTL543 was the very last to go, although the type lasted a little longer in learner service and as Aldenham staff buses. Many of the displaced Country Area RTs were repainted red so that they could take over from roof-box versions. Some Routemasters also found themselves displaced. They were not, of course, withdrawn but moved on to remove RTs from passenger service.

And so by the end of December 1968 the London bus fleet was looking markedly different to that of a year earlier. It would change very much more in 1969, although it would quickly become clear that the Merlin was falling far short of its expectations.

1969

To start on a cheerful note and record an innovation which was to prove durable, the extension of the Victoria Line to Victoria itself took place on 7 March 1969. It was a great occasion. HM the Queen performed the opening ceremony. Royalty is not often found beneath the streets of London and no reigning monarch had ever taken part in such a ceremony before. The Victoria Line proved even more popular than had been predicted. The journey time between Victoria and King's Cross was reduced from 24 minutes to ten and by the summer the line was carrying passengers at the rate of 58 million a year.

Up above it wasn't the new generation of single-deckers which provided the first Central Area OMO conversions of the year, rather the RF which replaced Sutton's RTs on the 80A. However the Merlin onslaught resumed with a vengeance in May and continued through to October at Bromley, Muswell Hill, Enfield, Loughton, Alperton, Hounslow, Potters Bar and Plumstead garages.

The reason the Merlins did not appear earlier was that they were fully occupied in the Country Area. In February they arrived at Hatfield, Windsor, St Albans, Garston and Hemel Hempstead garages, while RFs followed the examples of their brethren at Sutton and ousted RTs at Dunton Green and Dartford. Next month more Merlins went to Windsor.

There were many who felt that the building of a large fleet of Green Line double-deckers was flying in

Left:
RF431 of Sutton at Morden station.

Left:
MBS407 of Crawley works a local service in the town centre.

Left:
RMC4 was among the Routemaster coaches which were sent to work as buses from Hatfield garage. This far outlived its prototype brethren in ordinary passenger service; it is seen here inside the garage.

Right:
Heyday of the red Routemaster – a line up at New Cross garage.

Below:
Pictured in Addlestone in 1994, SM3 was one of the 1969 deliveries of Swifts and the last of its generation of AEC single-deckers still working regularly in the London area. This was AML's first purchase, in 1992, hence its title.

the face of experience and common sense, and within four years of the last RCL entering service the first RMC was demoted to bus service. On 15 February route 708 was reconverted to RFs and the RMCs which had worked this service from East Grinstead and Hemel Hempstead garages could find no employment elsewhere on the contracting Green Line network. So they went to Hatfield, and later in the year Addlestone – briefly – and Grays, where they took up bus work, replacing RTs.

October saw the last Merlin deliveries. Excluding the 15 experimental vehicles of 1966, 650 had been put into service in the extraordinarily short time of 13 months, between September 1968 and October 1969. It was an unlucky 13 with a vengeance, for the type was nothing short of a disaster. When one considers

how thoroughly the prototype RTs and RMs had been tested before going into production, one can only wonder what on earth possessed LT to invest so much in an unproved design. It is true that one-man services needed to be introduced quickly in order to cut costs, but the Merlins saved little and the RTs soldiered on for another 11 years after the Merlin's introduction, outlasting them all – except for the Red Arrow vehicles, which outdid the RTs by one year, while the Routemaster is, of course, still with us. The last non-Red Arrow Merlins were taken out of traffic by the end of 1976.

One of their principal liabilities was their length. Looking back it seems somewhat naive that it was felt that their troubles would be over merely by shortening them and fitting a smaller engine. Nevertheless this

Above:
Seen between the Gasworks and Copenhagen tunnels outside King's Cross BR station, an LT battery locomotive has charge of a train of Northern Line tube stock. A Class 47 is waiting to back down to the terminus whilst a Class 40 has just emerged in the right background.

was what happened. A 33ft 5in long version, the Swift, was ordered, again in very large numbers. The first, SM1, appeared in late 1969 and was sent to Catford garage. It had the same neat looks of the Merlin although the body was actually built by Marshall. This was the first time the Cambridge firm had built new bodies for LT, although it had taken part in the rebuilding programme immediately after the war.

RTs continued to be taken out of service as the big one-man single-deckers became a familiar sight throughout the LT empire, in both Central and Country areas. They in turn replaced many of the RTLs and RTWs in the training fleets although both types managed to last into 1970.

1970

If we continue to describe each year as 'particularly significant' or even 'traumatic' then you, dear reader, may well feel we are suffering from adjectival overkill. However we must take the risk and note that 1970 can lay claim to being perhaps the most traumatic of all years since LT came into being. For on 1 January the Country Area passed out of 55 Broadway's control and became part of the newly set up NBC while LT itself passed from state control to that of the GLC.

1,267 buses and coaches were handed over to London Country, as the former Country Area was now to be known. The first obvious sign of these changes was the new wording appearing in gold Johnson face capitals on green buses. The livery, for the moment, was otherwise unchanged. The new Swift single-decker had been ordered for both Country and Central Area services and, although they probably wouldn't have been London Country's choice, it was too late to do anything about this and anyhow the new concern was desperate to go OMO just as quickly as possible. The first green ones took up work in June 1970 from Leatherhead on routes 418/418A, followed in August by deliveries to Addlestone, Crawley and Guildford. Not only were RTs replaced but also the last of the green RLHs. One might have thought that these 53-seat double-deckers with their inconvenient lowbridge layout would have been replaced by the very first batch of high capacity single-deckers but they had managed to last into the new decade.

London Country's new symbol appeared in the early summer of 1970. It lacked the classic simplicity of the

traditional LT logo, being a solid circle, surrounded by an open one with what was assumed to be wings surrounding this. Some wit remarked that it looked like a flying polo and, not surprisingly, the name stuck; this was particularly appropriate for London Country was a peculiar animal having a vast hole in the middle of its territory, ie the red bus area. There were those who reckoned that such a geographical oddity was destined for a short and not particularly merry existence.

Croydon, always at the forefront of new initiatives of course, found itself host to the XAs which

inaugurated flat fare C1-4 routes between New Addington and Croydon, C1 being the express service, except on Saturdays when it became the C3 for the benefit of shoppers and ran along North End, the principal shopping street. FRM1 also arrived at Croydon and worked route 233 which served Roundshaw, a new housing estate with a spectacular see-through power station, built on part of Croydon Aerodrome. Croydon had been London's airport before World War 2 but afterwards, there being no room to extend the runways for the much bigger

Above:
The birth of London Country. The interestingly numbered RT4444 still carries its old insignia but the RT behind at West Croydon bus station has just received its London Country fleetname.

Right:
London Country's first Swift, SM101, in Reigate garage. Just visible behind it is a former M&D Harrington-bodied Reliance coach which London Country used as a trainer.

airliners coming into service, its importance declined and it was eventually closed. The 233 was London's very first OMO double-deck route, inaugurated by XA22 on 22 November 1969.

As host to some of the final batch of RMLs, the XAs and the FRM Croydon was the proud possessor of the most up-to-date fleet of double-deckers in London, although not all were equally appreciated. The RMLs and the FRM were fine buses but the XAs, despite being overhauled before being sent to Croydon, soon became know as 'rattle-boxes'. Worse was to follow.

The first Central Area Swifts, SM1-10/12, took up work from Catford garage on routes 160 and 160A on 24 January as part of yet another reorganisation of routes and cuts in services. Although shorter than the Merlins they were still longer than the RTs they replaced and this immediately caused problems, the drivers deciding to take a different route on the Middle Park Estate to that announced. In April the nearby Bexleyheath garage received Swifts, as did the west London garages of Fulwell and Hounslow, while the final batch of SMs arrived at Cricklewood in June. All the SMs seated 42.

Before this the first SMSs had entered service. The SMS was a two-door version of the Swift. It had 33 seats, mostly in the raised, rear portion and room for 34 standing passengers. The entrance on the left was for passengers who preferred the human touch and wished to pay the driver; that on the right was for the technologically minded with the correct fare who pushed it into a slot which they were misled into believing would then instantly send a message to a turnstile to let them enter the magnificent interior. It mostly did, but sometimes it didn't and of course even a few failures got the apparatus a bad name. Most passengers preferred to pay the driver which did nothing to speed things up.

The London Country Swifts, although dual-door, did not suffer these problems as all passengers had to pay the driver. The SMSs introduced a third body builder of the large capacity OMO single-deckers, although one more familiar to London than any other, Park Royal. Marshall, MCW and Park Royal bodies were built to very close specifications as regards appearance and, whatever the failings of the actual vehicles, they were neat and well proportioned.

Route 70, previously operated by RTs from New Cross, was the first SMS route, the conversion taking place on 18 April. Next they went to Edgware, taking over on 13 June, a day long-remembered for the utter chaos they caused; passengers and staff seemed quite unprepared for their arrival to the extent that someone had forgotten to order paper rolls for the automatic ticket machines. In September SMSs and new route 82 were introduced between Hounslow bus station and London airport, although it would be some years yet before RTs disappeared from Heathrow routes. On the last day of October SMSs replaced their longer brothers at Enfield.

The conversion I best remember also took place that day, when Croydon, Thornton Heath and Elmers End garages received the type. At that time I was regularly travelling on route 194 and one could hardly say the new single-deckers were received with unalloyed joy. Apart from sentimentalists like me who were simply fond of the RT for its own sake, the general public liked neither having to queue up to pay the driver before they could board the bus nor then finding they had to stand when they were properly inside. Many decided it was more comfortable to wait for a 54 or 119, both routes still worked by RTs, and often quicker as the double-decker would catch up and overtake the SMS laboriously loading up at a stop down the road.

The last Swift conversion of 1970 was the 226 when seven were sent to Willesden garage and took up work on 7 November.

The huge RT fleet, numbering 2,775 scheduled for service in January 1970, was in rapid decline now and by the end of June all those without heaters had been withdrawn from passenger service. None had been built with these comforts and when they began to be fitted it was decided that no roof-box bodies, these generally being the oldest, would have them. One did, the Saunders body on RT1903, by mistake so it is said. This lasted out 1970, but otherwise the roof-box body, so distinctive a feature of the London bus, was now gone for ever from passenger service. Some remained a little longer in the training fleet, but the last of the Leylands used in this capacity and as staff buses, RTLs and RTWs, were all withdrawn in 1970, although some stayed delicensed with LT until the very last was sold in April 1971.

No RTs received complete Aldenham overhauls after the beginning of 1970 and even standard RTs with heaters were now being sold, but repainting went on and some RTs received the now standard RM fleetname with all the letters of equal size and no underlining.

In September 1970, a new design of surface car, the C69, began to enter Underground service. A total of 212 vehicles were built by Metro-Cammell, sufficient for 35 six-car trains with one spare two-car unit. It was now possible to use identical types of vehicle on both the Circle and the Hammersmith and City lines; 14 trains took up work on the former line, 17 on the latter. Each six-car train consisted of three two-car units, with a driving cab at one end of one of the cars. One of the curious problems which has always affected Circle Line trains is that, apart from giddy drivers, the wheels wear unevenly. So, every so often one is sent to Whitechapel which ensures that when it returns to the Circle Line it is facing the opposite direction: devilishly clever.

By 1970 the dangers of smoking were becoming apparent – we shall arrive at the horrors of the King's Cross fire later – and instead of 50 per cent of the cars allowing this, only two in each six-car train were so designated. This rather complicated matters as no three units stayed together for very long, so the no smoking signs had to be moveable. The C69 stock – so designated because it entered service in 1970 –

looked rather like its immediate predecessors, the A stock. However there were many differences, notably the provision of four doors in each carriage instead of the three used on the essentially outer suburban As; all measurements were in metric although this hasn't as yet seen any units transferred to the Paris Metro. The arrival of the C69s saw the end of those antiques dating from the 1920s, the Q stock. I used to travel regularly in these on the East London line at that time and marvelled, as we rattled past what remained of the London docks, at the plethora of swaying leather straps hanging from the clerestory roofs. It was 1971 before the very last was taken out of service. Several were preserved, notably driving motor car No 4248 which can be seen in the LT Museum at Covent Garden.

1971

The inexorable, although far from all-conquering, march of the one-man single-decker continued through most of 1971. However its replacement had already appeared at the 1970 Commercial Motor Show and it began work in London on 2 January 1971. Keith Hamer wrote a piece for the *London Bus Magazine* entitled, 'The Good, the Bad and the Dodgy', which precisely encapsulated the career of the DMS. In 1970-1 I had a part-time job teaching photography at Tower Hamlets College of Further Education, and one evening, after slaving away over a hot enlarger and talking to the rather engaging daughter of a dock engineer and the son of an Afghan chief, on my way home to sylvan Oxted I bought a copy at London Bridge of the *London Transport Magazine*. In its pages I learned all about its wonderful new bus, the DMS or Londoner, as it wished to be called. No one had ever thought of giving such a grandiose title to the original B, the STL nor even the RT. A little later I took my students for a ride in one on route 5 down Commercial Road and we got roared at by the driver for over-riding our stop, which taught me that one-man drivers took the conducting side of their two-man duties seriously.

Anyway, the *London Transport Magazine* was fulsome in its praise of 'London's Bus of the Future', as one would naturally expect and I must say it looked rather nice, though not everyone thought – or thinks – so. It was much better than the XAs and the XFs, which were its ancestors. The Daimler XF Fleetline, having performed better than the Leyland XA Atlantean, was chosen as the basis for London's next generation of double-deckers. Until 1966 the law had demanded that all double-deckers have conductors, hence the Merlin and Swift single-deckers, but these, as we have seen, were far from satisfactory, and when the law was changed LT set about adapting the DMS to its requirements. Because of the bus grant from the government, which defrayed up to 25 per cent of the

cost of a new vehicle providing it was to a manufacturer's standard design, and because British Leyland wasn't prepared to produce a one-off for LT, the standard Fleetline chassis with a Gardner engine was chosen.

LT had bought its last AEC. The last Regent came off the production line in 1968, as the final

Above:
Two Hammersmith Line trains of C69 stock pass outside Paddington.

Below:
DMS111 in Commercial Road.

Left:
Catford's (TL) RT4795 and Elmers End's (ED) SMS821, George Street, Croydon.

Below left:
RLH49 at Stratford shortly before withdrawal of the class.

Right:
The ceremonial last steam train on the Underground comes into view near Swiss Cottage, seen between a Bakerloo Line tube train and a Metropolitan Line A stock train.

Routemasters were being delivered, and the Merlin and Swift single-deckers were a sad final chapter in what had been, for the most part, a glorious story – the collaboration between AEC and LT stretching back to the earliest days of the motorbus. The excellent Reliance continued in production and was chosen for the Green Line fleet until the very end, which came in 1979, when the works closed with the loss of over 2,000 jobs.

Just as London had ordered huge numbers of Merlins and Swifts without proper trials so, partly because of delivery delays, it did the same with the DMS and, surprise, surprise, ran into equally horrendous problems. Would you believe 1,967 were on the order books before the first had entered service. If the chassis was 'off the peg', the body was LT's own. There was a front entrance, divided so that passengers could either pay the driver or use the automatic machine and turnstile; the exit was amidships. There were seats for 44 upstairs and 24 downstairs with room for 21 standing passengers. The livery was the dullest yet seen on a London bus, red all over; thank goodness for adverts! AEC might be gone but Park Royal was still in business and it built the first DMS bodies. Tram replacement route 95 and trolleybus replacement route 220 were chosen to receive the first DMSs on 2 January 1971. As great a contrast as one could imagine was the RLH. This lowbridge double-decker seated only nine more in all than the DMS did on its upper deck alone. The last few managed to hang on into the DMS era, being withdrawn from Dalston garage and route 178 on 16 April.

Because of their vastly greater seating capacity, passengers were much happier with the DMS than with the new generation of single-deckers. Also, it has to be said, with the end of the overhaul cycle which had ensured an RT emerging from Aldenham was as good as new, these veterans were becoming distinctly shabby, inside and out.

Like the Merlins and Swifts the early DMSs had a public address system but it was little used and later

ones were not so fitted. DMS76 was given a broad white band above the lower-deck windows, which improved its appearance somewhat, and this became standard from 118 to 367. Meanwhile Chiswick Works fitted two instead of four-leaf entrance doors to DMS240 and painted them bright yellow (the surrounds, not the glass). This, together with a solid white bullseye logo instead of the rather insipid open one which was replacing the LT legend, was to become standard. The white stripe was omitted.

Decimal currency arrived more or less concurrently with the first DMSs – on 21 February 1971, to be precise as far as LT was concerned – and so all ticket machines, whether conductor-operated or automatic, on buses and of course machines at all Underground stations, were changed on that day, a massive though

Right:
Former GWR pannier tank, London Transport No L94 at Finchley Road, 7 June 1971.

worthwhile undertaking. DMS delivery continued right through 1971: RTs, RMs, Merlins and Swifts all being replaced, although only the RTs were actually withdrawn as a consequence.

Congestion was still growing, both in central London and the suburbs, but the socialists in charge of the GLC at County Hall were sympathetic to public transport and between 1970 and 1975 increased bus lanes from three to over 100. The steadily increasing number of OMO buses certainly didn't speed up traffic but was seen as the only way of holding down costs. It was expected that eventually conductors would disappear from the London scene and with them the now elderly RTs and the much newer Routemasters. LT had hoped that the larger capacity of the DMS would mean that it could operate rather fewer buses but because they spent so much longer at stops than the RT and the RM they soon had to settle for a one for one replacement policy; indeed on some routes more vehicles had to be scheduled when open rear-entrance buses were replaced. OMO was truly a necessary evil.

Royalty returned to the Underground when the final section of the Victoria Line to Brixton was opened by HRH the Princess Alexandra on 23 July 1971. Work was now well under way on the extension of the Piccadilly Line to Heathrow, sanctioned by the government in November 1970. Rather remarkably, although steam had disappeared from British Rail in August 1968, it survived on LT for another three years, former GWR pannier tanks continuing to work in dwindling numbers on engineers' trains. By the spring of 1971 only three remained and the end came on 6 June when a special last run was made over the Metropolitan between Barbican and Neasden by L94, formerly No 7752, hauling a train of engineers'

wagons. Large crowds turned out all along the route to watch; rather surprisingly, no one seems to have got themselves electrocuted and, 1971 being well into the preservation era, No L94 then headed off for a new lease of life on the Severn Valley Railway. A number of its fellows were also preserved and LT, realising the potential of all this, has since run many specials, hauled both by the preserved electric loco *Sarah Siddons*, and various steam engines, over the Metropolitan. It can honestly be said that steam has never really gone from this unique section of the Underground system.

1972

In order to ensure that all RTs and RMs could be replaced by 1978 (ho, ho, ho) that other stalwart LT body builder, MCW, began to produce DMS bodies, the first arriving on DMS1248 in March 1972. As with the RTs the two body builders were given separate blocks of numbers, thus the high number of the first MCW bus. Engines for the DMS were supplied not only by Gardner, but there were also a few from Rolls-Royce – very up-market. Of course, as we all know, you pay for quality and the Rolls-Royce engine proved to be a good deal more expensive to run. Neither did the name Rolls-Royce automatically mean higher quality any more than a minibus based on a Mercedes chassis guarantees a superior turn of speed. Following the addition of Daimler to the Leyland fold, and a shortage of Gardner engines, Leyland engines

Below:
DMSs, SMSs and one distant RM at Brent Cross.

were also fitted to Fleetlines. At first they were very noisy to the extent that, after the original DMS so fitted, No 1250, had been delivered in March 1972, the others were either put in store without engines or were given Gardner ones until the problem had been solved.

Although full scale overhaul of the RT had ended, recertifications and repainting still took place. By now only one RT route, the 197, was still operated by Croydon garage but evidence that the class was alive and kicking came in the spring when a number of members of the class emerged gleaming with a new coat of paint, which put members of the already shabby SMS class, alongside which they worked, to shame.

Meanwhile the problems besetting the OMO single-deckers continued. Some were already out of traffic but the entry of MBS4 into Aldenham for a pilot

overhaul in June 1972 suggested that perhaps the class had a future. Virtually all the Merlins had been repainted by the end of 1972. Some variations on the standard livery were carried out, while MBA606 appeared covered in an overall advert – a phase LT was beginning to go through at this time – for Chappell's music store.

The last of the Swifts arrived in March 1972. By then it was obvious that the smaller engine, necessary on account of the reduced length of the bus compared to the Merlins, was very unreliable. It had been uprated but was still considered under-powered by many drivers. The automatic heating system was inadequate – there being insufficient warm air in winter, insufficient cold air in summer. I remember a particularly miserable ride in a Swift on route 115 through Purley on a damp winter's evening, although

the packed bodies of the steaming, standing passengers did help to heat things up a bit. Paintwork became less than pristine far too early in the vehicles' career and various body defects soon made themselves apparent, although these, just to make life even more interesting, varied from manufacturer to manufacturer. Repainting of Swifts began in October 1972 and, like the Merlins, there were some experiments, chiefly featuring variations of white, which, generally, improved the buses' looks.

Out in the wilder reaches of the Home Counties, ie London Country, great changes were afoot. Under the old regime secondhand vehicles were practically

unknown but the almost bewildering change around, which has become such a feature of modern bus fleets, had begun in 1971. Fifteen AEC Swifts, the SMW class dating from 1969-71, with bus bodies built by Willowbrook and Marshall, were transferred from South Wales Transport in 1971-2. The first three had uninspiring Willowbrook 48-seat bodies; the rest 53-seat Marshall bodies. These were built to the much more handsome standard BET specification, and were very similar to M&D and Southdown buses which they sometimes encountered in the course of their duties. Another Swift variation was the SMA. These also should have gone to South Wales but all 21 were

Above:
St Albans city centre with London Country Reliance RP2 of St Albans (SA) on the 727 and Garston's Atlantean AN103 on route 321.

Left:
GS55 in London Country ownership.

diverted to London Country before delivery. Very different in appearance, they had a double Celtic connection for their bodies which were built by Alexander in Scotland. They were put on Green Line service and had 45 coach type seats and spent most of their lives working route 725. The SMAs replaced RFs which were now being withdrawn.

None of the rear-engined Swift variations was really successful; the underfloor Reliance was vastly better, although in its early days this too had its problems. The first of the 90-strong RP class, Park Royal-bodied, 45-seat Reliances, basically buses but with coach type seats, went into service at the very end of 1971, on the 727. The rest arrived in 1972 and quickly replaced practically all the RMCs and RCLs in Green Line service. The only exceptions were three RCLs which Godstone retained for the rush hour and Sunday 709. This was drama indeed. Splendid as the Green Line double-deckers undoubtedly were, the doubting Thomases had been proved right. OMO, large capacity single-deckers were far more appropriate for the Green Line network of the 1970s.

The RT class was severely reduced in 1972, numbers being cut by around two-thirds. But a surprise was the sale of 34 RTs in September – to LT. New Year's Day saw RCLs arrive in Croydon on route 414 and the companion 405 got them on 25 March.

Now that I was living in Oxted, Godstone and Chelsham were my local garages and the former hit the headlines early in 1972. I was nosing around in the tin shed on the corner of the A22 and A25 at the end of January when I came across a brand-new OMO rear-engined double-decker, London Country's very first, painted in mid-green and a nasty mustard yellow

livery. Yet another Celtic exile, it was a Northern Counties-bodied 72-seat Daimler Fleetline originally intended for Western Welsh. In all there were 11 of these AF class buses, and they took over from Routemasters on the 410, popping up on the 411 on Sundays.

Before spring 1972 was out another new class of OMO double-decker, one destined to be much more numerous and long-lived than the AF, appeared. This was the Leyland Atlantean, the AN class which is still with us. The first 90 had handsome Park Royal 72-seat bodies; the last 30, yet another diversion this time from Midland Red, were given similar MCW ones. They, too, appeared in the new green and yellow livery and brought about the end of great numbers of RTs. The first went to Hertford garage chiefly for routes 310 and 310A, and were soon a familiar sight in Croydon, being sent to Chelsham, Leatherhead and Guildford for the 408 and 470. By the end of 1972, 237 RTs had been withdrawn, most for breaking up although some found other owners.

The livery which London Country had chosen was rendered obsolete almost before the paint was dry, for by the autumn of 1972 the stranglehold of the NBC had dictated that, just as with the old Tilling companies, every concern within its huge empire should paint its buses either poppy red or leaf green and adorn them with its double N symbol and fleet name in corporate style. Thus the later Atlanteans appeared in this guise.

The vehicle most associated with the early days of the NBC was the celebrated Leyland National. This single-decker, still a familiar sight throughout the land, was intended to be Britain's standard bus for generations and had been developed by British Leyland in conjunction with the NBC. Not everyone would use the adjective 'celebrated' to describe it, but it is certain to become, if it isn't already, a classic bus design, the Model T of the bus world. London Country was destined to own more Nationals than any other bus company, in Britain or abroad. I met my first one autumn afternoon at Chelsham where it had arrived for crew training. It had a rather impressive front; from the side I thought it less attractive, while the pod on the roof at the rear, which contained heating and ventilating equipment, looked all the world like an old fashioned luggage rack.

As the first Nationals arrived so the last of the little GS normal control buses were taken out of service from Garston garage, when their last route, the 336A, was withdrawn. By 1972 we were well into the preservation era and, apart from some which continued on PSV work with other operators, a number have been restored to their original pristine 1953 condition.

The Victoria Line at last was complete in every detail when Pimlico, featured as the station for the Tate Galley on the north bank of the Thames, opened in September 1972. Meanwhile a new design of tube train was entering service on the Northern Line. It was very similar to the Victoria Line stock, which by now numbered 316 vehicles, but was designed for crew operation. 90 driving motor cars, 90 trailers and 30 uncoupling non-driving motor cars were ordered from

Metro-Cammell. Withdrawal of the prewar, red-painted stock began with the delivery of the 1972 stock. Although this is now long gone elderly trains of 1956/9/62 stock can still be found on the Northern line.

1973

The rate at which the RT was being withdrawn suggested it would not see out 1973, certainly with London Country and perhaps not LT either. But this remarkable vehicle was not that easy to dispose of and LT took only 260 out of service that year, while London Country switched its withdrawal emphasis to the RF. At the end of 1973 there were still well over 1,000 licensed for service with the two concerns. One RT which did disappear that year was No 4325, the very last roof-box one which had been operating as a trainer until 9 November.

If the RT, dating back to 1939, was still needed; the Merlin, dating back to 1966, wasn't. The pilot overhaul of MBS4 had taken no less than eight months; the Certificates of Fitness for the class were coming up to expiry. Experience had shown that there was still a need for the double-deck bus whether crew or one-man operated, and all this, combined with the general unreliability and unpopularity of the Merlin prompted the GLC to announce in August that it sanctioned its gradual withdrawal.

Below:
Metro-Scania MS5 at Clapton. *Author's collection*

Right:
Saunders roof-box RT2343 on learner duty in Tottenham.

Below:
The LT Collection at Syon Park with LT165 prominent.

The prototypes had all gone by October 1973 and the first 15 production buses, MB16-31 were taken out of traffic; the rest lasted the year out.

Production of the Merlin's replacement, the DMS, continued in considerable numbers throughout 1973, although there was a hiccup when chassis production was transferred from the old Daimler works at Coventry to the Leyland one at Farington, Leyland. To most enthusiasts, Farington instantly brings to mind the final Leyland body design for the PD2, which bore this name with such distinction. By 1973 the once revered name of Leyland had become something of a musical hall joke, as the unreliability of its products

and periodic shortages of parts had reached epidemic proportions. Despite having a virtual monopoly of the British bus industry, and one or two excellent products, there was widespread dissatisfaction at its performance. The seeds of its own doom were being sewn and the market was being got ready, however unintentionally, for mainland Europe manufacturers.

One industry in which Britain has excelled in the latter part of the 20th century is that of exploiting its history, and not just olde worlde Anne Hathaway-type cottages, castles, cathedrals and such, but equally successfully its industrial heritage. The cynical might claim that, as we have become steadily less capable of making and selling products for home and foreign consumption, so we have excelled in demonstrating how good we used to be. It's rather more complicated than that: all of which is a roundabout way into recording the transfer of the LT Collection to Syon Park.

The Clapham Museum had been closed and the British Rail exhibits transferred to the magnificent new museum which was due to open at York – a laudable move away from London's monopoly of all things bright and historic but this left London's historic buses, trams, trains etc, looking for a home. Syon Park, belonging to the Duke of Northumberland, is beside the river between Brentford and Isleworth and on the opposite bank from Richmond, a very nice setting, if not terribly central or handily placed for public transport. The collection was housed in a modern building, and opened by the Duke on 23 May. Among the exhibits not seen at Clapham were two from the Underground, Q23 Metropolitan District car No 4248, and Metropolitan electric locomotive No 5 *John Hampden*, both only recently withdrawn.

If the Merlins were giving trouble the Swifts were no better, probably worse. Large numbers of them were unserviceable at various times throughout 1973, a combination of their many inherent design faults and shortage of spare parts from British Leyland. A vastly more successful single-deck class appeared in 1973. The local east London route, the S2, received six Leyland Nationals, LS1-6, in November. These were the precursors of a large fleet, many members of which are still at work in London, of which more anon. They worked alongside six Metro-Scanias, MS1-6, which had arrived a little earlier. These, too, were to have a considerable influence on LT policy in the years to come, although the vehicles themselves did not last long in the fleet.

Yet more variations on the single-deck theme had appeared in 1972, delivery continuing in 1973. Apart from the livery and LT roundels the vehicles of the FS class could not have looked less like the traditional London bus for they were tiny 16 seat Ford minibuses. They had bonnets and were thus the first

Left:
Ford Minibus FS11 on the B1 in Bromley.

Below:
Leyland National LN7 on Superbus duty at Stevenage in the company of an Atlantean and a United Counties Bristol/ECW RE.

Above right:
Bakerloo Line 1972 tube stock at Willesden Junction.

normal control red buses since the Leyland Cubs and were basically converted vans – 'Bread Vans' as the breed was instantly dubbed. They operated experimental services, at the request of the GLC, for a 10p flat fare, mostly along roads out in the suburbs which until then had never been served by public transport.

Congestion was getting steadily worse throughout London, and the GLC – sympathetic to public transport – continued to introduce bus lanes. Oxford Street west of Oxford Circus had been closed to ordinary traffic between 11.00 and 23.00 in October 1971, an experiment which led to the permanent exclusion of all except buses and taxis, while the most famous bus lane, the contraflow one along Piccadilly allowing buses to run from the Circus to Hyde Park Corner, came into operation in April. By the end of the year there were 45 in operation during the morning and evening rush hours. BESIs (Bus Electronic Scanning Indicators), looking like leftovers from an episode of *Doctor Who*, appeared at intervals along selected main routes which were able to monitor the position of each bus, direct radio links with drivers had begun in 1971, while Computer Assisted Radio Location Aids (CARLA) were introduced in 1973. These automatically pinpointed the position of every bus on a particular route. All these innovations were attempts to combat congestion and delays, although vandalism and assaults on crews were growing and there was an element of attempting to come to terms with this unpleasant phenomenon too.

The great London Country event of 1973 was the large scale entry into service of the Leyland National. The first four were already at work, on the Stevenage Superbus network, LNs1 and 2 carrying K suffix registrations, the rest being NPD-Ls. The first to appear in green livery took up work from Dunton Green on 1 January 1973; many others followed for bus work throughout the network.

The next innovation was the appearance of Nationals in Green Line guise, RPs being replaced on route 721 in February. From the outside they looked rather handsome in their two-tone livery, but internally, where it mattered, they were a disaster. One wonders just what aberration persuaded London Country's master, the NBC, that the PVC-covered bus seats would be acceptable to passengers, particularly as the almost new RPs which they replaced had proper coach seats. Nevertheless more of the same was provided, although later ones did have a moquette covering but the seats were still basically bus ones and the National was quite definitely a bus, not a coach.

At the other extreme five proper coaches, the very first Green Line had owned, did enter service. Plaxton Panorama Elite II-bodied AEC Reliances, they were painted in standard NBC white coach livery and were used solely for private hire and tours. They were given no class or fleet numbers and were known only by their registration numbers, SPK201-5M.

The RPs moved on to other Green Line routes and these and the Nationals wrought havoc with the RF fleet which by September had no scheduled allocation on Green Line routes, other than from Chelsham on the 706. However RFs would pop up with perhaps not surprising frequency on Green Line services for several years yet.

It could only be a matter of time before the ECW/Bristol combination, so beloved by the nationalised companies, joined London Country; the breakthrough happened in October. While single-deckers and coaches had been growing longer and wider there remained a need for something a good deal smaller, in the tradition of the C and GS classes, and so London Country ordered a fleet of 35-seat ECW-bodied Bristol LHS6Ls – the BL class. They provided a further assault on the RF class which lost 63 members by the end of the year.

More new tube trains entered service from November. This was very similar to that of the previous year and was known as 1972 Mark II stock. There was a striking variation in the livery, the doors being painted red. The LT roundel, already appearing on buses, now appeared on trains. The large scale production of both marks of the 1972 stock meant that the long familiar 1938 stock now began to be withdrawn and scrapped.

1974

Withdrawal of LT's Merlins began in earnest in 1974; London Country would keep its fleet intact a little while longer. Indeed, in order to cover its chronic vehicle shortage, a number of LT's Merlins were hired out to London Country, a situation which continued to December 1976. The assault on the Merlins meant that although more than 400 DMSs joined the fleet, they mostly took over from the single-deckers. RTs were removed from four routes in January, 1974, but after that the type was left largely undisturbed so that only 118 members disappeared from the fleet that year: the drastic spare parts shortage resulting from the three-day week was one reason for this.

Not only were many RTs still needed but plans eventually to turn the fleet over to entire OMO were being put on hold, if not yet abandoned. In recognition of this it was decided to put a number of Fleetlines into service with conductors and class them as DMs. Some DMSs were already fulfilling this role, albeit with their OMO equipment intact. The first DMs proper took up work on route 16 from Cricklewood garage, replacing crewed DMSs in September, 1974. There were to be 400 DMs in all, numbered DM918-1247 and 1703-1832. The thousandth member of the class, DM1000, was the subject of a handing-over ceremony at Park Royal at the end of the year.

One of the routes which did lose its RTs was the 197, Croydon garage's last one. It had operated the type for over 26 years, since the very earliest days of the postwar RT when they had arrived in large numbers to replace the Tilling and General STLs and the STs which had more or less monopolised Croydon's routes. RTs were still to be found in the town, notably from Chelsham, Catford, Bromley, Thornton Heath, and Brixton garages, the two latter putting them out on the 109, the busiest route on the entire LT network.

Up north, on 19 October Dial-a-Bus began, operating amongst the leafy avenues of select Hampstead. Although the basic outline of the route, starting from Golders Green, was fixed, passengers could make bookings to the controller at Golders Green or hail the bus, an FS 'Bread Van', and it would make diversions to pick them up, providing they were not waiting in one of the many cul-de-sacs which Hampstead Garden suburb boasted.

Leyland had originally intended that the National would be produced with as few variations as possible in order to ease its production and keep costs down.

Below:
Newly overhauled RT537 in Croydon garage in May 1972.

Just how it expected to maintain this rigidity is a puzzle, presumably it was devised by an expert in systems theory rather than a student of human nature; British Leyland certainly didn't seem to have employed anyone versed in the quirks and idiosyncrasies of bus passengers and operators. However it began to learn its lesson quite early on and in August 1974 a new version for Green Line service arrived fitted with proper coach seats and luggage racks. The series began at SNC116, WPG 216M. The S stood for short, the National being produced in two lengths, 33ft 10in and 37ft 2in. The longer ones were, naturally enough, given an L prefix.

A variation on the BL class appeared with London Country in August. This was a 7ft 6in wide version, and it was initially put to work along the narrow lanes of Surrey, Kent and Hertfordshire. Designated BN (N for narrow) the 30 members of the class went to Northfleet, Chelsham, Dunton Green, Dorking, Guildford, Leatherhead and Hertford garages, replacing RFs.

Although we are primarily concerned with vehicles we cannot ignore the wider context in which they operate and this might be an appropriate moment to consider some of the factors which determined the type of vehicles and their operation in the mid-1970s.

The cooling of enthusiasm for OMO, typified by the arrival of the DM class, is spelled out in the introduction to the LT 1974 Annual Report and Accounts: 'The problem of ticket issue and change giving, which increase [sic] the time that passengers take to board vehicles on heavily-used routes is one of the factors that limit – at least for the present – the number of buses that can be single-manned under London conditions.' Over 60 per cent of buses were still crew-operated. In a year when total passenger journeys were up by 1 per cent and staff shortages were down, although 'there was a shortage of skilled engineering staff,' a considerable restraint on progress was caused 'by a shortage of serviceable vehicles . . . delays in deliveries of new buses and . . . a severe shortage of spare parts for the bus fleet.'

The report then goes on to refer to the energy crisis and the 'staggering increase in oil prices. The fuel used in the Executive's electrical generation stations at Lots Road and Greenwich had sustained a more than fourfold price increase in nine months.' A particular statistic which sticks in my mind from this time is that the fuel oil being used by the great liner *France*, then on a cruise, had doubled in cost between the beginning and ending of its voyage. It was shortly after taken out

Left:
SNN138 at Chartwell, Sir Winston Churchill's former home whence route 706 was extended in summer. In the background is an elderly Bristol/ECW L5G.

Left:
RMC1480 of Dartford received an all-over advert for the Co-Op in 1974. It is seen here heading down the A23 for Brighton passing the preserved Southdown Leyland G7 of 1921 taking part in that year's HCVC run.

Left:
DMS1 after its first overhaul and transfer to Merton garage.

Above:
The approach to Ealing Broadway with two District Line R stock trains on the left, BR parcels car passing the Greenford Loop DMU in the sidings and a Paddington-bound express double-headed by two Class 50s.

1975

of service, to be bought subsequently and re-engined and converted to the *Norway*.

Nothing as drastic as re-engining was proposed for London's bus and train fleet, but it was hoped that the steep increase in petrol prices would curb private motoring. For a brief period in December 1973 when there was a petrol shortage: 'bus mileage lost because of traffic congestion had dropped dramatically by 50%.'

The GLC had a policy of keeping fares down, highly commendable too, but difficult to sustain with such a dramatic increase in fuel costs. In November the GLC had accepted 'that there must be a major increase in fares' (they were to go up by a staggering 56 per cent in 1975). The report went on to note that there was: 'a recognition that the cost of providing an acceptable public transport system in London must be borne by the public one way or another, if not as fare-payers then as ratepayers and taxpayers.' This argument has been central to political debate, both at national and local level, ever since, the emphasis swinging first one way, then another. At its deepest level it reflects how one views society and how great a contribution the richer should make to improve the lot of the poorer. Though usually seen as a question of Right versus Left, it can cut across party lines and leaves many bus and train enthusiasts confused, torn between wanting to see a properly funded public transport network which invariably means a high degree of state control, but objecting to the uniformity and standardisation that this often entails.

In the spring of 1975 the first general fares' increase since 1972 took place, most bus and Underground tickets costing a third more. The cheapest 3p fare went up to 4p, the 5p to 7p, the 12p off peak maximum remaining, while the maximum at other times, 20p, was reduced to 15p. Red Arrow fares doubled to 10p. It was hoped that an additional £35 million would thus be brought in.

Two tragedies, different in scale, but both traumatic, clouded 1975. In January a conductor on a 77C bus, Ronald Jones, died as a result of an incident involving two 21-year olds. Both LT and London Country buspeople (no longer busmen for women were now driving London buses) had been protesting over the rising number of assaults on crews, and these protests increased dramatically, amidst much public disquiet about the situation. The press seized on every incident and there was a good deal of over-dramatisation and harking back to a supposed non-violent golden age, even if no one could quite recall when precisely this was; but for all that operating a bus in some parts of London and the suburbs had certainly become more hazardous. High level talks involving cabinet ministers, union leaders and the Chairman of LT took place; the police were given increased powers, and alarms and radios were to be fitted to vehicles.

On 28 February 43 people died when a Highbury branch Northern line tube train, instead of coming to a halt in Moorgate station, careered through it and crashed into the dead end tunnel just beyond. Carriages were telescoped and it took many hours for all the injured and dead to be extricated from the horrendously mangled wreckage. The driver was one of those who died and there has never been a

satisfactory explanation of the accident. Somewhat ironically the branch closed later in the year in preparation for it to become part of the Great Northern section of British Rail's suburban electric network.

1975 was the year the RT was supposed to be taken out of service but hundreds were still needed and three-year re-certifications and some repaintings were the order of the day. Only one OPO conversion to DMS, route 183 at Hendon garage, took place, although other RTs were replaced by two man DMs and Routemasters.

It was the Merlin which, as in 1974, was the chief target for withdrawal. All the two-door MBs had gone by April and so rapid was the Merlin's disappearance that LT had to store them on the disused Radlett aerodrome. A total of 350 had gathered there by the end of the year, a rather extraordinary sight from passing trains on the Midland main line out of St Pancras.

Just about every bus company except LT was operating ECW-bodied Bristols of one sort or another and although the Lodekka never became a familiar sight on the streets of London – come to think of it that's not true, for Eastern National and Thames Valley examples did have regular workings on express routes into London but you know what I mean – LT jumped on the bandwagon in 1975 when six little 26-seat LHS6Ls arrived. Put into the BS class they were sent to Highgate to take over from the FS minibuses on the C11. They were painted in traditional red with white surrounds to the window frames and looked rather fetching. They were also adorned with the now almost white bullseye logo. RTs were the only class never to receive this, keeping the traditional gold underlined fleetname or, in a few cases, the later unlined version. Not everyone approved of the white roundel. It was my opinion that it simply showed how dull the old style had been. I know Gill Sans was ideal

for destination screens, clear and easy to read, but for a fleetname it was pretty uninspiring, not a patch on the handsome General which it replaced or, indeed, the very nice Stagecoach now to be seen on Upton Park's Routemasters for example.

After that dizzying leap into the past and then to the future, let us return to 1975. The shortage of buses, old and new, showed no sign of easing; if anything it was getting worse. BEA, along with its Routemasters, had become part of British Airways in 1973. Not all received the new corporate livery and those that didn't, 13 in all, were sold to LT in August 1975. They were classified RMA and were rushed into service, still in BEA orange and white, with no route

49

indicators, merely a board in the nearside front window, and put to work from North Street garage on route 175. They had been given bells and used ticket boxes but no internal stanchions for passengers to hang on to and were clearly only a stop gap. They were re-certified and repainted into LT livery and lasted on passenger work until September 1976. Their story, however, was far from over.

As if orange wasn't a sufficiently different colour, 10 bright blue and cream double-deckers were next to join the fleet. These were handsome Massey and East Lancs-bodied Leyland Titan PD3s with exposed radiators, hired from Southend. Fortuitously they had three-piece indicators and were sent to Croydon, fitted with TC garage plates and from 22 September graced the streets of my home town on route 190. There was a sudden upsurge in the sale of sunglasses at Boots in North End Croydon around this time for, along with the red LT buses, the various shades of green of the London Country ones, and the Southend Titans, three more PD3s, this time ex-Southdown ones with Northern Counties bodies still in traditional Southdown pale green and cream livery, took up work on the 409 and the 411 from Godstone garage. London Country was having as many problems keeping its vehicles on the road as LT. There was yet more to come.

In order to replace its RTs on driver training duty, London Country bought 20 more Titans and painted them bright yellow. Undoubtedly the most famous of the many varieties of PD3 were the full fronted versions owned by Southdown and Ribble and it was from the latter company that the 20 trainers had come. By a remarkable coincidence both found their way into the London Country fleet and more than once I saw examples side by side at Godstone garage.

This was by no means the end of London Country's hirings and secondhand purchases. Only 30 new vehicles arrived in 1975, all Nationals, and, apart from hiring Merlins from LT, Bristol MW coaches came from Royal Blue and were sent to Dunton Green. As this garage worked the 483 to Croydon it is possible royal blue contributed to the kaleidoscope in the town. A second shade of yellow was certainly seen on some Bournemouth Corporation Fleetline double-deckers which worked in on route 408. Elsewhere on the London Country network there were single-deck Bournemouth Daimler Roadliners, brown and white Leyland Titans from Maidstone Corporation and blue and cream AEC Regent Vs from Eastbourne. Finally on the subject of London Country liveries we must record that two RTs still working in the training fleet, Nos 2230 and 2367, were repainted in National green.

The first section of the extension of the Piccadilly Line to Heathrow opened as far as Hatton Cross, serving the cargo terminal, in July 1975. New trains had been ordered from Metro-Cammell, hopefully for delivery in 1973, and they were designated 1973 stock, but in fact the first didn't enter service until the Hatton Cross extension was opened. They were some 6ft longer than previous tube stock, which they resembled in appearance. The red doors were abandoned but instead the front below the driving cab windows was painted red. In total, 196 driving cars, 175 trailers and 154 uncoupling non-driving motor cars were ordered. Because of the increased length of the cars they were made up into six rather than seven-car trains. There were a number of improvements and alterations compared with the 1972 stock but they still carried guards, rather than the one-man operation inaugurated with the Victoria Line.

Below left:
One of the 1977 delivery of ANs, AN157 bearing 'Watford Wide' logo, at Garston with derelict Swifts in the background.

Above:
A Bournemouth Corporation Daimler Fleetline on hire to London Country outside Leatherhead garage in the company of London Transport RT4286 and London Country former Green Line RF79.

Right:
A train of 1973 Piccadilly Line tube stock passing a District Line R stock train near Stamford Brook.

Left:
MD154 at Woolwich.

Below:
Crawley garage in March 1976 with, left to right, derelict RF and MBs, AN71 in all-over advertising livery, RCL2249 and former South Wales SMW1. NBC livery was now becoming widespread on London Country vehicles.

1976

1976 saw the sad Merlins disappear from all but the 500 series Red Arrow routes. They were all eventually sold, a good many for breaking up, but a lot found new owners. With them their careers varied; some lasted no longer than they had in London service but a few went on and served honourably for many years. This curious, almost inexplicable pattern was to be repeated with many former London buses from now on. In earlier times, certainly until the 1950s, London buses seldom worked as PSVs once their London service was over. The last prewar generation of buses and coaches had rather broken this tradition, and the postwar RT class, which had begun to be withdrawn as early as 1955, found ready buyers, not only in Britain but abroad too. These classes had, however, already proved their quality and reliability in London service. What was curious about the generation of OMO buses disposed of prematurely by LT, was that the reception they received from their new owners varied so greatly. We will look at this phenomenon a little later in relation to the DMS. Which brings us back to this somewhat ill-starred bus

By 1976 it was proving as troublesome as the Merlins and Swifts. Among many problems were the engines which frequently overheated, while the gearbox was a disaster. The two-man DMs, which it was hoped would not only replace the RTs but the RMs and RMLs too, were significantly slower in operation than the older buses on account of their doors, and had to hand back such routes as the 16 and the 24 to Routemasters.

An attractive new livery, with white upper-deck window surrounds, appeared and the Daimler badge disappeared on new deliveries, the bus being now known as the Leyland Fleetline.

Meanwhile a new type of double-decker, the MD, entered service on 21 March from Peckham garage on the 36; I saw my first one outside Paddington station on my way back from spotting some of the last 'Warship' diesel-hydraulics and leapt aboard to try it out. With its white upper-deck window surrounds, the two-level windscreen, the rectangular headlamps, the chrome lower deck strip, the nicely appointed interior and the significantly lower noise level, I thought it a distinctly superior class of bus.

Although there were only 164 MDs and they were not very long-lived, they heralded the death, long drawn out though it was, of British Leyland. With so much dissatisfaction with that company's products, there was clearly room for other manufacturers and the MD was an integrally constructed vehicle built in Birmingham by Metro-Cammell and fitted with Swedish Scania-Vabis running units. They were the first such mainland European-powered buses to run

in any quantity in London service. The entire class was allocated to the inner southeastern suburban garages of Peckham and New Cross and was generally to be found working the 36 group of routes, the 53 and 63. The last was delivered in February 1977.

Perhaps initially pleased with its MDs, LT announced late in 1976 that there would be no more orders for DMSs.

As in many other parts of the country the enthusiasm for dual door single-deckers soon waned and it was decided to convert a number of the SMs to conventional, single-door operation with increased seating. 42 seats were fitted and over 100 SMSs were dealt with, although not all actually re-entered service. The centre doors were simply sealed with a bar with 'no way out' painted on it fixed across them. It was crude and far below what LT would have tolerated in the 1950s.

Above:
Hounslow bus station with three
Leyland Nationals and RF536.

Right:
Routemasters replace RTs on route
109. RMS1449 and 1608 alongside
RT3559 and DMS1689 in Thornton
Heath garage.

Right:
A DMS overtakes FRM1, both working the London Sightseeing Tour, followed by an RM in Trafalgar Square.

Below:
Grays SNB218 of London Country at Grays bus station alongside an Eastern National FLF with a Southend Corporation Fleetline in the distance.

As 1976 drew to a close LT owned close on 1,000 unserviceable buses, an horrendous state of affairs. Coaches had to be hired, as in the early postwar years, to help fill the breach, though after union opposition they only ran on two routes. The first of a batch of 51 Leyland Nationals began to arrive in May 1976, ostensibly as stopgaps while the problems with the Swifts were resolved. They were sent to Hounslow garage, being joined there by the original six in order to keep the type together. Over at London Country the much vaunted Superbus network at Stevenage was in trouble partly because Stevenage garage had to operate such a diversity of types.

By the autumn it was clear that the Leyland National, as London Country had discovered, was a much more reliable bus. As many as 24 Swifts were withdrawn in October, one being almost immediately sold to some unsuspecting soul in Fiji. At the end of the next month LT announced the Swift would follow the Merlin into oblivion. In December the GLC gave LT approval to buy 50 more Nationals.

Meanwhile the RT proved it was still needed and, to help fill the gaps, odd examples were allocated to a number of routes through the heart of London, from which they had officially been banished some while back. For all that the newest member of the class was 22

years old and their numbers inevitably continued to decline. In May they at last began to disappear from route 109, first from Brixton garage and then from Thornton Heath. I had ridden this route ever since I had replaced the 16 and 18 trams in 1951, 25 years earlier. A quarter of a century is an enormously long time for one type of bus to operate a route, in London or anywhere else, although it is a record which Routemasters have emulated on a number of routes since. Many of the RTs from both Streatham and Thornton Heath looked tired and ill-kempt with patches of exterior paintwork completely worn away in the worst cases, and that once magnificent interior still serviceable but much faded and discoloured with upholstery threadbare, a state far removed from the pristine condition in which they had been kept in earlier days.

The only new buses to enter service with London Country in 1976 were Nationals. Many types moved around as a consequence and the numbers of RTs and RFs in service was minuscule compared to their halcyon days. Scheduled RT operation was now in single figures, a mere seven, while the RF situation was scarcely better, just 10. Rather more than this were actually needed but clearly they were not going to last much longer.

1977

1977 was Silver Jubilee year and LT, as always at times of national rejoicing, rose to the occasion. Much the most up-front manifestation of this was the repainting of 25 RMs into silver livery. Silver-painted buses blossomed throughout the realm; London Country, for example, produced two silver Atlanteans, one of which, AN5, in the early part of the year was regularly seen passing through, and indeed stopping, at Oxted; the other, AN41, inhabited the frozen wastes of the North.

The 25 silver RMs were temporarily put into their own class, the SRM. I saw my first one at Waterloo in April, appropriately on route 1. The sun was out and it looked dazzling. Inside the SRMs were carpeted in pure wool, I kid you not, a wonderful touch made possible by the International Wool Secretariat (no connection with Southdown, baaa, as far as I know) and the British wool textile industry. The design on the carpet incorporated the Woolmark, the Celebrations Committee emblem and the LT Silver Jubilee symbol. The latter also appeared on the side of the buses alongside the legend 'The Queen's Silver Jubilee London Celebrations 1977'. The SRMs worked on many of the routes which passed through central London, Oxford Street seldom being without at least one, and often several at any time of the day. There were those of us who felt that it would have been a nice touch if 25 RTs could have been chosen

for the honour, the RM not yet having reached the cult status it now boasts, but in retrospect the right decision was surely made. The RMs honoured were from the series 1648-1922.

While on the subject of RTs, 1977 was not a happy year for the class. Its brief return to central London routes to help out RMs was now finished, while the last daytime route into central London to which it had been allocated in full, the 155 from Merton, went over to RM operation in January. Nevertheless RTs were to pop up in ones and twos more or less regularly on routes 1, 12, 29 and 47 right through the year and into 1978. By the end of 1977 the number of RTs scheduled for service was down to 236 on 16 suburban routes and two night ones from Barking, the N95 and N98, Monday to Friday.

Just about everyone assumed that 1977 would be the last year for the London Country RTs. Nineteen were still at work at the beginning of the year but their five-year certificates were all due to expire. You may thus imagine my astonishment when, standing at the bus stop by Redhill station waiting for a 410 one afternoon in April, what for a moment I was convinced was an apparition in the form of RT1018 hove into view. I don't think I had ever actually rubbed my eyes before to check they were functioning correctly but I did now. RT1018 gleamed in a coat of just applied

Below:
Two LT Silver Jubilee Routemasters in Oxford Street.

National light green, complete with all the appropriate insignia and grey wheels. One elderly lady stuck her hand out in the hope that this vision would deign to stop but it swept past on its way home to Chelsham. I assumed it was returning from overhaul at either Crawley or Reigate but records indicate this was carried out at Northfleet, so I don't quite know why it was returning in such a roundabout manner; perhaps it had been sent to Reigate for approval.

The National livery, whether red or green, then and ever since has found little favour amongst enthusiasts. When one thinks of some of the magnificent colour schemes and insignia it obliterated – of London's immediate neighbours Southdown and M&D immediately spring to mind – how right we were. Yet the new image sported by RT1018 won almost universal approval. Next month similarly-adorned RT3461 joined it, to be followed in sunny June by RT604. One wondered where this would stop but that was it. The three took up work on the 403 and sometimes on the 453 and many was the pilgrimage made from all parts of the Home Counties and beyond to view their magnificence. One suddenly realised

how dowdy the old Lincoln green had been. It had worked well when there was plenty of white or pale green to offset it but once from 1950 onwards there was nothing to relieve it beyond a thin cream band then it was pretty uninspiring. I never liked the vivid yellow London Country had introduced to go with Lincoln green, but National green might have been designed for the RT.

Inevitably RT604, HLX 421, became just about everyone's favourite. For, while all RTs were veterans, this was really old, nominally belonging to the very first batch of Country Area RTs, delivered to Hemel Hempstead garage in July 1948, 29 years earlier. I saw one or other of the magnificent three most days, but their final fling was brief, for in September RT1018 and 3461 were relegated to the training fleet. However RT604 continued to work from Chelsham into 1978. Reigate also had an RT, No 981, still on passenger duty, although this retained the old Lincoln green and yellow livery.

A total of 157 new vehicles joined London Country in 1977. Seeing that just about every other fleet in the country owned some ECW-bodied Bristol VR double-

deckers, it was inevitable that 15 should be delivered to London Country. Originally intended to take over route 403, these highbridge vehicles of the BT class actually went to Grays for the 370. Their career with London Country was brief. More Bristols, this time further members of the BN class, 14 in all, also arrived.

A somewhat curious new class, the RN, turned up. These were 10 Plaxton-bodied AEC Reliances, built for Barton in 1972. Although they had coach bodies Plaxton had somehow squeezed in three plus two

seating, giving a capacity of 64. London Country put in some luggage pens, which reduced seating to 60. As the class was regularly used on school runs it's quite possible the pens served other purposes too. Their other sphere of influence was the 418, operated by Dorking garage.

More Leyland Nationals arrived, swelling the ever growing numbers of this class, but the event of the year was the introduction of the very first, out and out coaches to serve regularly with Green Line. These were 30 Reliances. They were put into two classes.

Above:
RT1018 on its first day in service in National livery at Chelsham working the 403 express, 6 April 1977. To the right are two former Ribble PD3s in yellow trainer livery.

Right:
The Queen opens Hatton Cross Piccadilly Line station. *LT*

RS1-15 had Plaxton Supreme Express bodywork built in Scarborough, RB16-30 had Dominant II bodies built by Duple in the former Burlingham factory at Blackpool. Originating as they did from the seaside they were in the tradition of proper coaches as used on long-distance routes patronised by day trippers and holidaymakers, with high backed seats, full length luggage racks, forced-air vents and individual reading lamps. They were put to work on a variety of routes, immediately moving the Green Line image on to an altogether higher level and proving popular with passengers – even though, as with so many modern coaches, leg room was rather less generous than it might have been. As a consequence of the arrival of these coaches, many Leyland Nationals which had served in this capacity were down graded, and none too soon, to buses.

1977 saw the end of London Country's first Reliance class, the comfortable but unreliable RC, and the return of some of the hired vehicles to their owners. The four former M&D Harrington-bodied Reliance trainers, T1-4, were also taken out of service in 1977.

In contrast to the celebrity status LT afforded the RM, London Country's Routemasters were in a state of decline. Withdrawals began in October with 2 RMLs, RCLs and RMCs being taken out of service. Many had been unfit for a while and were to be seen dumped in corners of various garages, sad and neglected. Grays in particular was a last resting place for these once cosseted vehicles. LT took a very different view of the Routemaster's future and by the end of the year had bought back 16 from London Country, with many more to follow.

Meanwhile the final version of the DMS, the B20 appeared with a redesigned rear end and a much quieter sound. Older ones which were due for overhaul were taken out of passenger service, some being used as trainers. Only two, DMS1 and DMS118 had so far received overhauls, at Aldenham, the pair emerging from a very lengthy process in March and October respectively.

The long-established Round London Sightseeing Tour was always likely to throw up something out of the ordinary, none more so than the unique former Midland Red D9s, hired from Obsolete Fleet Limited.

which had operated in open-top form since 1975. Seven convertible Weymann-bodied Daimler Fleetlines, the DMOs, were bought by LT from Bournemouth Corporation, now Yellow Buses, ready for the 1978 season. Another tourist attraction was route 100 which worked through the heart of the West End and provided me with my first ride on a Tilling ST since the 1940s for it was operated by the preserved ST922, also owned by Obsolete Fleet.

Merlin and Swift single-deckers were disappearing rapidly from the LT fleet, the only members of the former still at work being MBAs on the Red Arrow routes, but while Swift withdrawals also continued some of the class were recertified for another three years. More of the successful Leyland National and Bristol LH single-deckers were added to the fleet, the former reaching 107 members, the latter 95. These later LHs were longer, and placed in a new class, the BL. Many more Nationals were on order.

Below ground the big event was the opening of the Piccadilly Line extension to the centre of Heathrow Airport on 16 December. This didn't put road links with the centre of London out of business, which was no wonder for the tube extension was very much a compromise. Compared with what other European capitals offered, and Heathrow then as now was the world's busiest airport, it was a poor thing: a tube link which also served a considerable swathe of suburban west London, stopping at every station before the weary traveller from Tokyo, San Francisco, Birmingham, etc, was finally deposited in the West End.

On the surface lines a new version of the C69 stock, the C77, was put into production and, remarkably, actually entered service in the year of its designation. Although numbering only 11 cars C77 stock allowed

considerable alteration in the pattern of operation of the Edgware Road and Hammersmith & City services and meant that all C stock, whether on Metropolitan or District Lines, could be concentrated at Hammersmith Depot.

Above:
The last RF in traditional Lincoln green was RF684 of Chelsham which remained at work until May 1978. It is seen here heading across Limpsfield Chart on a bleak, February day.

Below:
RT436, nominally dating from October 1947, passing another RT on the North Circular Road at Edmonton.

1978

1978 saw the reappearance of green-liveried buses in the LT fleet. London Country Routemasters were now back on the streets of central London, although not quite in the pristine condition of their halcyon days of the 1960s. The RML buses were repainted and eight entered ordinary service in January alongside their brethren, which had always been red and from which they were indistinguishable. The former Green Line coaches took up work as trainers and, although they were gradually repainted red, many retained their green livery, but with the LT bullseye symbol, for several years. Others had been so robbed of parts that there was no possibility of them ever taking to the road again and they passed to that famous scrapyard, Wombwell Diesels, which if not in the sky was quite high up on the map of England – in Yorkshire, to be precise. Even so LT decided that it could actually save exactly half of the 38 which London Country had written off, while many parts were salvaged from the other 17 as they were being broken up.

As spring arrived the serviceable RMLs began emerging from Aldenham after a complete overhaul, rather than a quick repaint, their transmission altered from semi to fully automatic, and looking as good as new, inside and out. Nothing more vividly illustrated the different philosophies of LT and London Country – and both concerns, as is well known, employed a number of philosophers, full and part-time. While many of the RMLs which the latter disposed of in the late 1970s are still happily going about their business in central London and look set to do so into the next century, there are just two Routemasters in the possession of the many companies which once made up London Country, and these are cherished as vintage pieces of transport history.

1978 was the last year of London Country RT passenger operation. Reigate's No 981 went into the trainer fleet in February, leaving the celebrated RT604 to carry on at Chelsham. I stopped off at the garage one afternoon in June and found RT604 sitting in a corner at the back, all shipshape and shiny but minus one engine. Enquiries suggested that this would soon be restored but in the event it never was and so RT operation in what had been the Country Area of LT had finally ended. Astonishingly RT604 had seen it all, for it was one of the first batch delivered in July 1948 and had thus served for 29 years and 11 months; not a bad investment.

Time was also running out for the red RT. I had been taking pictures of this unique bus since the early 1950s but, as I realised how few opportunities were left, I took myself off to parts of London I'd never visited before to track down the last survivors. The last Enfield ones disappeared in January, many of Southall's went a few days later; then they disappeared from the North Circular Road with the conversion of routes 102 and 261 at

Palmers Green. They were still to be seen in some numbers in southeast London, bumping over the tram lines in Beresford Square, and speeding across the green open spaces of Woolwich Common and Blackheath. In April the RT lost four of these services, the 54, 89, 122 and 146. With the 54 gone this left just one RT operating in Croydon, London Country's RT604.

Also that month route 105 gave way to RMs from Shepherd's Bush and Southall. Perhaps surprisingly the veterans could still be found alongside Jumbo jets and Concorde at Heathrow – but not after 15 July when RTs disappeared from route 140. The last RTs departed from Catford and Bromley garages on 26 August and now there were just two routes left, 62 and 87, both worked by Barking. They had also worked the night services, the N95 and N98, but crews, feeling safer with doored vehicles, had had them replaced by DMSs at the end of May. One of the vehicles at Bromley was RT422, a favourite of mine for it had long been nominally the oldest bus in London service and had served for a good while from

Below left:
RT4681 of Plumstead climbing Academy Road, Woolwich.

Below:
An elderly gentleman alights from Kingston's RF481 at Esher on a snowy March morning in 1978.

Thornton Heath garage. Even now its career wasn't over for it was transferred to Barking.

The intention was that both Barking routes would lose their RTs in October. The 87 did, RMs taking over on 28 October. However route 62 crews raised several objections to the larger Routemasters and so the RTs remained for the rest of 1978 and, indeed, still put in appearances on the 87.

Two completely new classes of double-decker entered LT service in 1978. Prototype Leyland Titans had been undergoing extensive tests for some time. The second, registration number BCK 706R, most closely resembled the production vehicles. Various proposals for a completely new design of bus exclusively for London service had come to nothing and the Titan was the next best thing, a Leyland design with much LT input. A total of 250 were on order and the first batch entered service from Hornchurch Garage on 4 December. The body, built by Park Royal, was of distinctive design, with lower-deck windows larger than the upper ones and a curious rear end. It possessed the now standard front entrance, centre exit and central staircase layout. There were 44 seats upstairs, 25 downstairs and room for 20 lucky standing passengers. Originally entitled the TN it actually entered service as the T.

The other new bus was the Metrobus, or M (originally MT). Based on the MD, it was built exclusively by Metro-Cammell. It bore a strong resemblance to the MD but had a front-mounted

radiator. It seated 43 passengers upstairs and 28 down. Both the T and the M had Gardner engines and these two classes would become London standards. The T was originally concentrated in East London, the M in the west. The first Ms entered service from Cricklewood on the 16 and 16A.

Both types, although their numbers are somewhat reduced, are still familiar in many parts of London.

In the single-deck fleet Leyland National numbers had reached 267 by the end of the year. Other new buses were five Ford Dormobile minibuses, FS22-6. If the RT was almost gone, it had been intended that the RF class would go a year earlier. By the spring of 1977 it was working only two routes, the 218 and 219, appropriately from the heartland of the single-decker, Kingston. They stayed on here only because anything

longer on the Kingston garage inspection pits restricted the way through the bus station. There being no immediately obvious solution to this problem, 25 RFs were recertified, some of them losing their LT fleetnames and receiving the white roundel and lettering. The RF remained in remarkably good condition, both inside and out throughout its long London career, better on the whole than the RT, and Kingston's last examples looked virtually new right up to the end.

London Country was gradually reducing its dependence on the RF throughout the 1970s, but it was in no hurry to get rid of this famously reliable vehicle. It still saw regular Green Line service and the last survivors wore a bewildering variety of liveries. Chelsham garage operated not only the last RTs, but

Left:
Titan T81 preparing to head back to Romford from a deserted Trafalgar Square early one Saturday morning on the N98.

Below left:
Metrobus M1 at Victoria alongside RM1676.

Right:
Crew changing at Barking, 16 March. In the distance are an RT, a DMS and an RM.

also the last bus RF in Lincoln green. This was RF684 which regularly came past the end of our road on one of the Oxted local routes. It lasted until 20 May 1978, but another RF, 221, a coach in full London Country bus livery, worked from Chelsham until October. This left just one, RF202, which worked throughout 1978 from Northfleet on both bus and the occasional Green Line duties.

1979

The RT finally bowed out from passenger service with LT on 7 April 1979. Ironically the first members of the DMS class, the successor but two of the RT, had already been withdrawn for scrap. Barking had not, until the last months of 1978, featured high on many enthusiast's lists of places of outstanding public transport interest, but now they came from far and wide to ride, photograph and, sadly in a few cases, steal items from the last examples of what had become Britain's most famous bus.

By re-routing the 62 it was now possible for Routemasters to take over. Six RTs were scheduled to work on the last day, a Saturday, and LT, aware of the great interest in the event, had produced posters and organised a grand parade. The very last to operate was RT624, nominally the oldest, having entered service as a roof number box green bus from Hemel Hempstead garage in August 1948. It was sheer coincidence that the last RTs operated by both LT and London Country were in the early 600 series. RT624 returned to Barking garage at 13.45, no doubt to the great relief of the inhabitants of the block of flats opposite Barking garage, the balconies of which provided rather too many grandstand views over the last few months.

At 16.00 the parade got under way, featuring the six RTs bearing in their route indicators the legend '1939-1979 final run of the RT bus'. Many other preserved RTs joined them but the most unexpected sight, certainly for me and for many others, was the bus which led the parade. This was none other than RT1.

The survival of this historic vehicle owed a good deal to chance. Strictly speaking, not all of it was the prototype of 4,824 others, for in June 1956 RT1's body had been fitted on to the chassis of former Craven RT1420. In this form it served as mobile training unit 1037J and lasted no less than 22 years. Sold in 1978 it was supremely fortunate that it passed into the ownership of that pioneer preservationist, the late Prince Marshall. Re-registered as EYK 396, he had it restored to the condition in which it had appeared in April 1939 with polished aluminium horizontal bands and 164A route blinds. This was its first public appearance after restoration and it looked superb. RTs were out on the road for a little while longer, as staff buses and trainers, but by the end of the year even these functions had ceased, although a few still remained in LT ownership. The end for the red RF had come just a week before the last RT ran. By transferring the 218/9 a few yards down the road to Norbiton garage, Nationals could take over. Seventeen RFs operated on the last day, 30 March, the last scheduled bus being RF507. Crowds turned out, the Mayor and Mayoress appeared, there were ceremonial runs and many of the last survivors went, not to the scrapheap, but into preservation. This phenomenon was now in full flood and practically 100 RFs are still in existence, in various states of repair, quite a staggering total.

Large numbers of DMSs were withdrawn throughout 1979, Fulwell becoming the first garage to get rid of its entire allocation. It took to its replacement, the Metrobus, with enthusiasm, and still

Left:
London Transport's last passenger-carrying RT, 624, prepares to take part in the farewell parade at Barking Garage on 7 April 1979.

Centre left:
RT1 in the RT Farewell Parade, Barking, 7 April 1979.

Bottom left:
Shoplinker RM2171, Hyde Park Corner.

Right:
Shillibeer-liveried RM2153, Oxford Circus, 16 March 1979.

owns a considerable number. By the end of 1979 357 DMSs had been taken out of service. Metrobuses and Titans were proving more reliable with 1,000 due to be delivered by 1980.

The DM concept with two-man operation was of limited use, so a number were fitted with driver-operated ticket machines and reclassified D. 1979 marked the 150th anniversary of the first proper bus service to operate in London, that of George Shillibeer, and DM2646, the newest Fleetline, was sponsored by British Leyland and repainted in a handsome livery of dark green and cream with appropriate lettering and insignia. At the same time 12 Routemasters were similarly attired, while the replica Shillibeer horse-bus, built at Chiswick by the LGOC in 1929 for the Centenary celebrations, reappeared, although presumably not with the same horses.

If the appearance of RMs in the striking Shillibeer livery wasn't sufficient, only two years after the 25 Silver Jubilee buses, then 16 appeared in another equally striking guise – the Shoplinker. This service began on 7 April and ran between some of the principal hotels and stores in the West End. The livery was red on the lower deck and roof, the remainder bright yellow. Inside music played on both decks, interspersed with advertisements, in several languages. The 16 buses operated out of Stockwell garage. Shoplinker was a nice idea but it failed miserably, the buses carrying few passengers, and the service came to an end on 28 September. One spin off was that Londoners were becoming used to seeing their buses in other than the standard red, which was just as well, for in the years to come every colour combination known to man, would be seen on the streets of London and its suburbs.

On 1 May 1979 London's latest tube line, the Jubilee, opened. Like so many of its predecessors it incorporated part of an existing line, the former Bakerloo section from Baker Street by way of Neasden to Stanmore. Completion was delayed by two years, hence its title, but the new section was worth waiting for, much relief being provided as an alternative route to Bond Street, Green Park and, above all, its Charing Cross terminus. It was never intended that this would be a permanent end, but the government refused to fund the proposed extension southeastwards and it was only in 1993 that this was finally put in hand, to Docklands and Stratford. It is to be hoped that no tourist boards a Jubilee Line train sometime in the future with the intention of finding Shakespeare's lil' ole birthplace.

New trains, the D stock, for the District Line entered service in 1979 and they remain the newest surface stock. Their arrival marked the end of an era as surely as did the withdrawal of the last RTs, for completion of its delivery in 1983 brought about the end of the careers of the famous CO/CP and R stock.

The D stock consists of 450 cars, made up of three-car units, divided into A, C, and D types. Normally an A and a D unit work together, with driving cabs at the outer ends of the train, although at the opposite end of each unit, ie facing each other, there are simple controls which can be used to perform shunting movements. The 20 C units have driving cabs at both ends so that they can substitute for either an A or a D.

The D stock was built to metric measurements and the cars were longer than their predecessors, approximately 18m (60ft) against 16m (50ft). Although

somewhat similar to the C69/77 stock, there are noticeable differences. The sides are flat but taper slightly in order to allow the greater length of the cars to negotiate all curves on the District Line. Although given the usual aluminium finish this was relieved by a red panel at the front of each unit below the cab windows A new system of door control allowed passengers to open individual doors, although the guard could over-ride this and, of course, was in charge of the closing of all doors.

The last prewar-designed CO/CP, red-painted trains were taken out of service in March 1981, two specials being run on the final day, 31 March. A number of cars from this stock has been preserved in various locations.

London Country was determined to try and make the Green Line network viable and to help with this no fewer than 90 new coaches were taken into stock in 1979. They were repeats of the previous year's Reliances with Duple and Plaxton bodywork, and were leased for five years rather than bought outright. The old style of operation with services starting out deep in the Country Area, passing through the suburbs, central London, out through more suburbs and terminating on the outer fringes of the Country Area was no longer viable in the traffic conditions of the late 1970s and the last such services ended in 1979, either being curtailed or split, each section terminating in central London.

Jetlink 747, linking Heathrow and Gatwick airports by Green Line, not Jumbo Jet, began on 28 April with the Reliances in a special livery; standard Green Line livery had already departed from the strict NBC guidelines. The RF just lasted into this era, the last one, RF202 based at Northfleet, still occasionally appearing on routes 725 and 726 until it was withdrawn in July.

The 90 Reliances which Green Line put into service were a remarkable statement of faith in a company which had produced the great majority of London's buses and coaches for eight decades. But the last produced for LT, the Merlin and Swift single-deckers had been a disaster; the rear-engined Routemaster had remained a sole tantalising example of what might have been, and even the last Reliances were called Leylands. On 25 May 1979 the AEC works at Southall closed.

1980

For the first time in our history we enter a decade without the RT. Around this time I attended a seminar given by one of LT's senior engineers at Chiswick Works. It was a fascinating experience; one could sense the hankering for the old days of certainty with a standardised fleet of Chiswick-designed purpose built buses. Few doubted that the Merlins and Swifts suffered from severe design faults and were unreliable, but was the DMS really equally disastrous? We were told that it was simply incapable of standing up to the demands of day to day service in London and that's why it was being prematurely withdrawn and broken up or sold. But I couldn't help wondering if all the fault lay with the DMS. Could it be that LT simply didn't understand that it was a different sort of bus to the RT and the RM and needed to be dealt with in a different way? By then ex-London DMSs were in regular employment in Birmingham, Manchester (and still are, some 15 years on) and Glasgow; were conditions in these rural backwaters so very different to those in London?

One use London did have for some of its DMSs was as trainers, and 40 were so converted during 1980. The DMS trainer is still an occasional sight on the streets of London, although not from the original 1980 batch.

London's first Swedish double-deckers, the MD class, were taken out of service in 1980. Their career had been brief and not wholly successful – corrosion and lack of spare parts had caused problems – but they had led the way to the highly successful Metropolitans. The withdrawal of the MDs meant that the 36 group of routes went back to Routemaster operation. This was not the first re-conversion from doored buses; that had happened in March 1977 when RMs returned to route 29.

In contrast London Country had just 13 licensed Routemasters at the beginning of 1980 and they had less than two months to go. Chelsham, which had operated the last RT, very nearly operated the last Routemaster, managing to find work for RMC1515 on the 403 express until mid-February. It was outlasted by RMC1512 at Swanley on the 477 by a couple of days. RMC1512 and RML2446 performed a farewell tour on 1 March but this was not quite the intended end: Swanley unexpectedly used RMC1512 the following week, on 4 and 5 March, on route 477, to substitute for an unfit Atlantean. Next day, 6 March, it and all remaining Routemasters went straight into LT ownership.

Despite being anxious to get rid of the Routemaster, London Country had kept its prototype, RMC4, in ordinary service far longer than LT did its three, and it worked from Hatfield until May 1979. London Country had no intention of parting with this very special vehicle as we shall shortly see.

Meanwhile LT decided to put 26 of the RCLs to work as ordinary buses. This was done with great thoroughness: the doors were removed, a stanchion and grab rails fitted, the double headlamps converted to single, and the luggage racks removed. They were sent to the former trolleybus garages of Stamford Hill and Edmonton to work route 149. I had a ride on one, boarding it at Victoria, and was most impressed, not only by its immaculate paintwork, without adverts, but also by the deep, Green Line seat cushions, which were retained.

Below:
London Country AN184 and RMC1501 on rush hour workings of route 403, West Croydon.

RCL2221 was converted to a cinema and exhibition bus. I met it at a number of rallies including, somewhat unexpectedly, alongside former GWR 4-6-0 No 6000 *King George V* at Old Oak Common depot.

1930 had seen the beginning of the Green Line network and 50 years later this important anniversary was commemorated in some style. A handsome book was produced, written by D.W.K. Jones and B. J. Davis with help from a number of authoritative sources. The frontispiece was a handsome colour photograph of one of the original Green Line coaches, T211, working the C2 at Sevenoaks and couldn't have been taken later than 1938. Rare indeed – prewar colour photographs of any PSVs hardly exist.

Back to 1980. A number of the latest coaches were adorned with a large gold band and lettered 'Golden Jubilee', and the celebrations reached a climax on Sunday 13 July when a commemorative run took place from Golders Green to Crawley. Some 150 vehicles

took part, many of them with close Green Line associations. There were five prewar coaches plus CR14 which worked Green Line reliefs, a huge number of RFs, many other postwar past or present Green Line coaches, and RT and RM Green Line double-deckers. A sign of the times was DMS631, one of six of this type which London Country had bought to use as trainers and had repainted in NBC green livery.

As pleasant a spot as Syon Park is, it had not been the ideal venue for the LT Museum, not least because it was a long way from central London. Therefore it was with considerable celebration that the museum moved into new premises in Covent Garden and opened to the public on 29 March. As in Syon Park there was nothing like enough room to display the entire collection, but against this the former market buildings were themselves a delight and the venue could not have been more central. Not surprisingly both visitor numbers and takings at the shop soared.

On 6 October the Transport Act (1980) came into

Above:
Restored Tilling ST922 working Vintage Bus service 100 to the new LT Museum at Covent Garden, seen in Trafalgar Square with Routemasters passing by.

force. This was the first step in the encouragement of competition in the transport industry which was one of the cornerstones of the Thatcher administration – although the evidence suggested it was more a question of political dogma rather than a planned policy. Now coach routes longer than 30 miles were deregulated and Green Line vehicles began to make regular appearances in places well beyond what had for long been regarded as Green Line territory: Cambridge, Oxford and Brighton amongst them. With AEC no more, Green Line had to find other chassis suppliers and two Volvo B58s and two Leyland Leopards arrived for evaluation.

The Merlins and Swifts of whatever type, buses and coaches, LT or London Country owned, were fast disappearing and, although a number were scrapped, a great many appeared with new owners literally all over the world. I came across considerable numbers of both types in Northern Ireland, particularly in Belfast and Derry. The Merlin was quite popular but the Swift was not and many of the 80 owned by Citybus and Ulsterbus saw very little service. Some, inevitably, were destroyed in the Troubles.

1980 went out on a rather downbeat note; for the first time ever no buses or Underground trains ran on Christmas Day.

1981

The all conquering Leyland National conquered the last of LT's Merlins in 1981 – the last London Country ones had gone the previous year. The MBAs, latterly with some help from SMSs, had clung on to the Red Arrow services long after the type had been forced to abandon all others, but their end came in the spring and early summer of 1981. They were replaced by 69 10.6m long, two-door National 2s. The National 2, with its front-mounted radiator and bulging front end, was instantly recognisable. Meanwhile the prototype and early production Nationals were being overhauled at Aldenham, a process which was deemed much more successful than that of the Merlins, Swifts and Fleetlines.

LT simply couldn't make up its mind what to do with the Fleetlines. The previous year LT had decided

they would have to last longer than had originally been intended and overhauls went ahead on the Park Royal-bodied examples. Then, in 1981, overhauls of Park Royal buses were abandoned and the previously despised MCW version was taken into Aldenham. The very last pre-B20 DMS of any persuasion to be overhauled, No 1987, a Leyland-engined MCW-bodied bus, entered Aldenham in December 1981.

Meanwhile the Titan was having problems. LT was a good deal happier with this bus than it was with the DMS family but it attracted few buyers elsewhere. Without these the bus wasn't really an economic proposition for Leyland. Additionally there were problems at the Park Royal factory, that long time supplier of so many London bus bodies, and it closed down in 1981. Titan production was moved from there to Workington, but the move drastically slowed down the number of buses entering service so that by the end of the year London had only 370 Titans against 700 Metrobuses – hence one reason for extending the life of the Fleetline. London Country continued to patronise the handsome standard Park

Royal body for its Atlanteans until virtually the end.

Now that the DMS was no longer regarded as totally beyond redemption, it was used to replace some of the last remaining Swifts. A few worked Red Arrow services until the Nationals arrived, but otherwise the last was SMS771, which was taken out of service from Edgware garage on 23 January 1981. The last Red Arrow Swift was delicensed on 27 July. The London Country examples lasted a little longer, but Nationals had replaced practically all of them here too. The very last, SMA1, was taken out of service on 1 January 1982.

The saga of the Merlin and Swift was a sad one for all sorts of reasons, not least that it helped bring about the end of AEC, although the way the entire Leyland empire was heading it probably wouldn't have survived much longer anyhow – unless it had emigrated to Sweden or changed its name to Dennis.

London Country's RP class, another AEC type, was now on the way out and it lost much of its Green Line work in 1981. By the end of 1981, 34 remained licensed, including four in use as trainers.

Above:
SMS700, drafted into temporary Red Arrow duty, speeds across Waterloo Bridge. It is a pity that such a neat looking design was so unsuccessful.

Right:
A derelict Swift awaits its end at the back of Norbiton garage.

The XF was a small class always associated with East Grinstead garage. The last, and the last former LT bus to work in normal service for London Country, was XF3. It, and its garage, ceased to serve London Country on 31 December 1981.

A few years earlier it had seemed that the Bristol, seen in huge numbers in so much of the United Kingdom, might come to play a large part in the affairs of LT and London Country. In the event its popularity was fleeting. London Country disposed of its VR double-deckers in 1980, many of the services operated by London Country's LHs disappeared along with the buses through lack of patronage and county council support, and LT's BS and BL classes remained intact for only a short while. In the late 1970s and early 1980s it sometimes seemed that the paint was barely dry on a new bus before it was whipped off to a Yorkshire scrapyard, an American theme park or perhaps a third world entrepreneur.

London Country continued to put its faith in the Atlantean, particularly the later AN68, and the National – both these types are still operated in some numbers by London Country's successors – while the Leyland Tiger was the principal replacement for the Green Line Reliances.

Above left:
DMS2512 working the short-lived 616 has the advantage over a Swift around Marble Arch.

Left:
Godstone garage with XF1 prominent; AFs, an RML and a National play supporting roles in the background.

Above:
LS77 in the foreground, three Swifts very much in the background, DMS1131 and DMS1134 alongside, Thornton Heath garage.

Right:
London Transport's loss is Santa Claus's gain. Preserved RT4497 on the last leg of its journey from Lapland delivers him to Oxted County school's Christmas Fair.

1982

From time to time we have noted the vast discrepancy in size between LT and all other such undertakings throughout the United Kingdom. A perfect example of this was provided in 1982 when LT put in its order for new double-deckers to be delivered the following year. The 150 Metrobuses and 210 Titans amounted to a quarter of all double-deck buses on order in the UK – and 360 was small by earlier London standards.

A legal judgement at the end of 1981 was to have a huge impact on bus and underground services in London and is still quoted as a landmark. For those who argued that it was essential for a modern city to have a co-ordinated public transport system sufficiently intensive, convenient, safe and cheap to wean people away from the private car so that restrictions on the latter would not merely be tolerated but welcomed, the decision of the House of Lords that the GLC had unlawfully raised rates in order to subsidise bus and Underground travel, was a tragedy. The challenge had come initially from Bromley; a borough at that time considered by many obsessed with tightening the purse strings however dire the consequences. In fairness Bromley did have a point in wondering why it should subsidise Underground and tube travel when no part of the network penetrated the borough. The GLC won in the divisional court but lost

on appeal. There was, inevitably, an element of party politics in all this, the Labour GLC being utterly opposed to everything the Conservative government stood for – and the Conservatives ruled Bromley.

Be that as it may, LT fares were generally doubled from 21 March 1982 and service cuts were planned. LT unions called the first general strike since 1926, and evidence was produced to show that, even taking into account the Fares Fair policy of the GLC, public transport subsidies in London were well below those of Paris, Brussels, Milan and New York. With the outlawing of Fares Fair the London subsidy fell to a derisory 12 per cent: Paris's stood at 56 per cent. As one who greatly admires the ever expanding public transport network in the French capital – buses, trams, Metro, RER and SNCF, I continue to be saddened by the short-sighted, miserable financial support Londoners and visitors to the capital receive.

Below:
M690 at Putney.

Right:
T119 in Piccadilly Circus.

Below right:
RM967 on route 11 pulls ahead of two open-top DMSs outside the National Gallery.

Inevitably the cut backs meant vehicle withdrawals and from 4 September 1982 some 500 less buses were on the roads during the peak hours. The first mass withdrawals of LT Routemasters took place, over 150 disappearing in August and September. The RM had been around over 20 years by then and its demise had been predicted long before, so in one sense it was no great shock. The Leyland-engined vehicles were the first to go. Many were scrapped but, as we shall see, changing times and the still sound condition of this remarkable bus meant that it was to have a far greater and more diverse afterlife than any other LT type.

A new type of double-decker entered service with London Country. This was the Olympian, destined to be the last new Leyland double-decker. As the successor of both the long-established Atlantean and, in a sense, the Titan, it had bodies by several makers, including ECW until it went out of business, Roe and Leyland. The Olympian remains the most modern type of double-decker in a number of the fleets which have succeeded London Country.

Left:
Open-top former Midland Red D9, OM1, working the London Transport Sightseeing Tour in Park Lane.

Below left:
A Berkhof-bodied Leyland Tiger BTL of 1985 at Victoria coach station working the Flightline 767 surrounded by the phenomenon of the 1980s, the double-deck coach.

Above:
A 1962 stock Central Line train leaving Blake Hall on the Ongar branch for Epping. *John Glover*

Atlanteans and Olympians also took over from what had been the first new class of double-decker delivered to London Country. So the AF, which like its predecessor – the front-entrance lowbridge STL – had always been associated with Godstone garage and route 410, disappeared from passenger service.

A development which would grow apace came into prominence in 1982. This was the takeover by London Country of a number of LT routes, following negotiations with the various county councils which subsidised them. All were out in the distant suburbs where the delineation between red and green bus routes had always been vague. There was also movement in the other direction: two of the routes in the traditional, north of the river 3xx green series, 313 and 347, passed to LT.

The vast increase in air travel, particularly by holidaymakers, continued to provide the Green Line network with much business, not just to and from Heathrow and Gatwick, but Luton as well. Some

services were run jointly with Southdown and Alder Valley. A particularly cheeky one – joint with Alder Valley – was the Flightline 767, which ran non-stop between Victoria coach station and Heathrow's three terminals, competing directly with LT's double-deck airbuses. Another encroachment into the heart of LT territory was the use of two closed and two open-top London Country Atlanteans which were subcontracted by LT to help operate the Round London Sightseeing Tour, complete in full red livery with LT roundels.

Open-top bus tours of London were, like airport services, a growth area. I suppose it was a sign of my advancing years but I had always associated open-toppers exclusively with the seaside and I found the notion of citizens from Japan, Australia, the USA, Stow-on-the-Wold and elsewhere wanting to be shown the sights of London from an open double-decker rather disorientating. Very silly of me, for the number of tourists to London has increased manyfold since the 1940s, providing much welcome business for LT. In 1982 they contributed some £60 million to LT's income. I regularly take parties of schoolchildren from deepest Dorset on open-top Routemasters and they are entranced with this unique view of the sights. Probably the first RM to be regularly employed on sightseeing duties was former Northern General, EUP 406B, converted by Obsolete Fleet, which took up this work – with its top on – in 1982, while a year later, following changed legislation, Culturebus started the first hop-on/hop-off service using some DMSs. Initially these had a closed top but the open-top version soon appeared. It was as though the DMS had been created for showing off London to tourists for it has since appeared on these duties in a bewildering variety of forms and liveries with many owners, and continues to do so today. Much rarer was the fleet of converted Midland Red-designed D9s – a unique bus, much beloved by enthusiasts. Known as the OM class, Christmas 1982 found sufficient hardy souls to warrant using them, topless, on tours of the decorations in the West End.

The most rural of the tube services, the Epping-Ongar section of the Central Line, taken over from the LNER, had never been exactly a money spinner and in December 1982 it was reduced to a peak hours only service, a replacement bus service being provided at other times. Was this the beginning of the end for the Ongar branch? Read on and we will see.

1983

At the beginning of 1983 a new ticket, introduced the previous autumn, was proving popular. This was the London Explorer. It was valid for one, three, four or seven days and allowed unlimited travel on buses and Underground trains on much, although not all, of the network. The one-day ticket cost £4.50p. As I write this at the beginning of September 1995, I have in my pocket a Travelcard which I used yesterday, covering not only buses and Underground but also all the British Rail (or whatever this week's name for it is) network, and which 12 years later cost me just £3.30p. No wonder the Travelcard, which appeared as such in

1983 (although the Waterloo and City Line, which would eventually become part of the LT network, was the only British Rail line included in the original scheme) has proved enormously popular and has sent passenger figures climbing.

The GLC, refusing to admit total defeat in its praiseworthy attempts to make public transport economically irresistible, managed to find resources to bring about a 25 per cent cut in bus and Underground fares in May – 'Just the Ticket' – without incurring legal wrath. The fare system was now based on a series of zones, which was proving highly effective.

The Routemaster, while its numbers continued to diminish, was also celebrated in 1983 as we shall shortly see. OMO spread, two central London routes being involved, when the suburban ends of routes 77A and 134 went over to this form of operation. By 12 April London garages no longer employed conductors. Two famous garages which closed altogether in 1983, to general regret, were Mortlake (M), chiefly known for operating route 9, its buses being particularly well maintained, and Riverside, Hammersmith (R), which provided a large

Below:
Mortlake garage.

Above:
Two trains of C stock, a D stock train and an R stock set, the last of which ran in 1983, District Line, Wimbledon.

Below:
RT2189 on the famous Chiswick skid patch.

proportion of the buses operating the most famous route of all, the 11.

1983 was LT's Golden Jubilee, and for the rest of this chapter we will concentrate on the celebrations which marked 50 years of the world's largest urban transport authority.

Special events were held all over the capital, amongst the most notable being a thanksgiving service in St Martin-in-the-Fields in Trafalgar Square, an Open Day at Aldenham Works and – probably the highlight – a Gala Weekend on 2 and 3 July at Chiswick and Acton works. Saturday the 2nd was a hot, cloudless day and LT, with the co-operation of many other bodies and individuals, put on a wonderful show. I brought my three boys up all the way from Dorset to have a ride, amongst other treats, on the famous skid pan. At least one RT was still employed for this purpose, giving me one last, short, spectacular journey in an LT-owned member of this famous class.

All sorts of one-off liveries appeared in Golden Jubilee year. Most appropriately, RM1983 was painted gold as was T747. Other double-deckers, including four Routemasters, were adorned in the 1933 livery of red and white with silver roofs and black lining and looked truly magnificent, emphasising how dull the virtually all-over red was. As it happened 1983 marked the beginning of the end

for this. When brand new and shiny the red looks fine, and the plethora of adverts which have always been a feature of the London scene, often enhance it, but I for one have no regrets that since 1983 liveries have become much more adventurous, although, of course, I hope – as I guess we all do – that the central London bus will always be predominantly red.

Many garages, or I should say many individuals with a real pride in being part of LT, took it upon themselves to cosset and take especial care of one particular vehicle, usually a Routemaster, and many of these

showbuses were to be seen at Chiswick on 2 July 1983.

With a proper sense of the rightness of things, Croydon and Thornton Heath were amongst the principal focal points of the celebrations. There was a press launch at the Fairfield Halls, Croydon; the gold RM entered service from Croydon garage; D2629 was painted in the chocolate and cream livery of Croydon Tramways to celebrate 100 years of the town's charter; 1933-liveried DMS1933 was renumbered DS1933 and took up work on route 64 and then the 109 from Thornton Heath; and several Croydon

Above:
The unique single-deck RM1368 alongside LS194 in red, white and black livery, Chiswick, 2 July 1983.

Left:
The line up of the four prototype Routemasters, Chiswick, 2 July 1983.

DMSs, along with buses from other garages, received gold waistbands.

Many of these were all gathered at Chiswick for the great celebrations. There was a certain amount of controversy over one feature, the line up of the first eight Routemasters. It was an imaginative idea, particularly as RM1 had been somewhat neglected of late – I had come across it in the Chiswick tunnel looking sadly down at heel some years earlier – but it was claimed that RM5 was not the genuine article, the real RM5 being out of service at the time and RM555 substituted. Personally I couldn't see what the fuss was about: because of the overhaul system used at Aldenham virtually no production RT or RM came out with the same identity or, indeed, with many of the same parts, as it went in. Of course the prototypes were a different matter, and these, although modified over the years, were clearly what they claimed to be.

A very curious Routemaster which I had never seen before was the source of much interest. This was the single-deck – I kid you not – RM1368. Its top deck had suffered damage and it had therefore been neatly cut down to form a slightly odd looking experimental vehicle based at Chiswick.

Many preserved London buses were to be seen as well as those from other sources, AECs featuring particularly.

A similar event was staged at Aldenham on 25 September. Immediately afterwards the not altogether unexpected but nevertheless dramatic announcement was made that Aldenham works would close and the future of Chiswick was under investigation. If both went it was estimated that some £18 million would be saved each year – but at the cost of some 3,000 men and women losing their jobs.

1984

Orders for new Titans and Metrobuses in 1984-5 would, it was said, eliminate the DMS, although, please note, nothing was said about getting rid of the Routemaster. As it happened, surprise, surprise, there was still a number of DMSs at work on New Year's Day 1986 and by then production of the Titan had finished, the last, T1096, arriving in November 1984, although the highest numbered was 1125.

No concern as large as LT, operating in a capital city, can expect to steer clear of politics; nor indeed should it if we understand the political process to be

decision-making involving all citizens. The Labour-controlled GLC, headed by Ken Livingston, had been a severe thorn in the side of Mrs Thatcher's Conservative government, one such thorn being an illuminated sign set high on County Hall which flashed out the steadily rising number of unemployed across the river to the Houses of Parliament. Legislation was therefore passed abolishing the GLC, and devolving power to the various boroughs. In this London became virtually unique amongst capital cities in that it no longer had one overall authority. It was feared many services it provided would disappear, one being the free bus travel for old age pensioners. After much argument the government agreed to provide free OAP travel outside peak periods. Oh to be a pensioner

in the Republic of Ireland where my parents-in-law take themselves off by bus and train all over the country, for precisely nothing.

A London scheme which did have the wholehearted support, philosophical and financial, of Mrs Thatcher was the transformation of Docklands from the once busiest port in the world to a yuppie paradise. A little surprisingly it was acknowledged that there would be a need for public transport and in the foreword to the 1983 *Golden Jubilee Book*, published by the *Daily Telegraph* in co-operation with LT and written by Oliver Green and John Reed, LT Chairman Keith Bright referred to 'the "super-tram" – a new light railway which will link the City with Docklands and the Isle of Dogs.' In the meantime, while this was

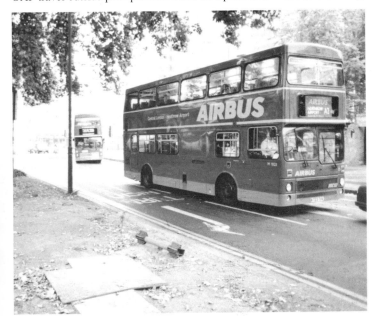

Above left:
TPL23, Green Line Plaxton Paramount-bodied Leyland Tiger at Hyde Park Corner.

Below left:
Green Line LRC3, an ECW-bodied Leyland Olympian coach from Northfleet, on the Embankment.

Above:
Another DMS finds a new owner, this time West Midlands. DMS1361 in New Street, Birmingham.

Left:
M1023 fitted with coach seats for Airbus duty at Shepherds Bush.

being planned, a bus service – the D1 'Docklands Clipper' – began on 3 January 1983 with financial support from the London Docklands Development Corporation. Using six LSs in special livery, it ran every 15 minutes from Mile End station through the new developments to the southern end of the Isle of Dogs, opposite Greenwich.

The world was changing – not that it has ever exactly stood still – rapidly in the 1980s and the winter 1983-4 edition of the *London Bus Magazine* commented, 'The London Regional Transport Bill, at present in its Commons' Committee Stage, looks as though it will be the biggest thing to hit public transport in London since George Shillibeer put his first omnibus on the road one hundred and fifty-five years ago.' This was some claim but, with the possible exception of the setting up of LT, it proved to be perfectly accurate, as the following chapters will reveal.

In passing we ought to note that the 1983-4 registration introduced the A prefix. Titans and Metrobus double-deckers carried it, as did three prototype ECW-bodied Olympians, L1-3, and three prototype Alexander-bodied Volvo Ailsa B55s, V1-3, all put into service in 1984.

Amongst the London Country vehicles with A prefixes were a batch of Leyland Tigers, the TP class, used on Green Line service and adorned with the newly introduced, finely proportioned Plaxton P3200 body. Possibly the most remarkable vehicles seen on a Green Line service since the RTC, or even LT1137, was the LRC class, which appeared in 1984 with A prefixes. These extra-long Leyland Olympians were fitted with ECW bodies, quite unlike anything the Lowestoft firm had previously brought out. All windows were fixed, the vehicles being air-conditioned, and 71 high-backed coach seats were fitted. With their extra-high upper-deck front windows, striped livery and generally streamlined appearance, they were not the sort of vehicle you could ignore. I never got to travel on one in Green Line days but I did have a ride in one with its subsequent owner, Northumbria, some 300 miles away beside the North Sea in Whitley Bay. With its fabric interior covering, luxurious seating and soft ride it was a most impressive machine. Would you believe it, these double-deck coaches did not prove ideal for Green Line work, hence Northumbria's acquisition of some of them. However examples of these Olympian coaches can be still be seen in London as I write, for M&D still have at least two employed on their Invictaway commuter services from the Medway Towns.

On 29 June 1984 the London Transport Executive ceased to exist and handed over to London Regional Transport (LRT). This was all part of the vast changes of the 1980s; a key aspect of the new philosophy behind the setting up of LRT was that services would be put out to tender. Just what this would mean in reality we shall see. Strong opinions were held on whether the LRT was a good or bad thing; time would tell, but one initially hopeful indication was an agreement between LRT and British Rail extending the Travelcard to BR services in London.

Below:
T833 dwarfed by the towering masts of the Cutty Sark, Greenwich.

1985

1985 opened with LRT (we soon went back to calling it LT) still committed to getting rid of conductors – and that meant the Routemaster, eventually – and extending OMO operation to 75 per cent of its routes by 1987. A new type of OMO double-decker appeared, the Dennis Dominator. The revival of Dennis is a remarkable and heart-warming story, the fortunes of this long-established Guildford firm waxing as those of the once dominant Leyland giant have declined. Way back LT had owned Dennis vehicles, both double and single-deck, although all had gone by World War 2. The Dominator was not, as it happened, destined to dominate in London in the 1980s but the success of Dennis single-deckers in and around London, and indeed elsewhere, has been truly remarkable.

The Green Line image was changing rapidly. The leasing rather than outright purchase of vehicles encouraged this and allowed constant modernisation of the fleet, a contrast to the years when the seemingly indestructible RF had held sway. The coaches really

Above:
Hounslow bus station. Three London Transport Ms and a DMS of London Buslines working tendered route 81.

Below:
Green Line Plaxton Paramount-bodied Leyland Tiger TPL73 stands in front of the impressive facade of Tunbridge Wells West station, terminus of route 706.

were just that, rather than buses with certain refinements. The Reliances dating from 1979 were replaced by Plaxton-bodied Tigers of the TP class and the lofty Berkhof-bodied BTL Tigers. The livery, a mixture of stripes and bands in two shades of green and white, was a good deal more attractive than either the old plain Lincoln green or National Express white. A number of Green Line coaches were painted in this latter livery and worked National Express services; some appeared on Green Line routes in National livery while conversely Green Line-liveried vehicles

could be seen hundreds of miles away from London on National Express work.

The subject of liveries will exercise us increasingly through the 1980s and into the 1990s. Those who thought that LT's Golden Jubilee year and Green Line's stripes represented the ultimate divergence from the norm would have been well advised to put in an order for several powerful sets of sunglasses. LT vainly, and schizophrenically, attempted to hold back the inevitable by forbidding one-off liveries for showbuses while allowing specific services such as the Docklands Clipper and two routes through the heart of London, 15 and 23, to carry special branding and bright yellow stripes. The ban on showbuses was never rigidly enforced and in a number of cases the buses were bought by the staff who had cared for them as the Routemaster fleet declined, RM1000 at Croydon for example.

More remarkable was the putting out to tender of some suburban routes. Thirteen were won by other operators, who replaced the former red LT buses with their own vehicles in liveries which ranged from the

bright yellow DMSs of London Buslines, which took over the 81 from Hounslow to Slough, through the standard National green of Eastern National's VRTs on the 193 from Hornchurch to Romford, to the ivory-coloured minibuses of Crystals, operating the 146 from Downe to Bromley North station. All carried notices with the LT roundel and the legend 'London Regional Transport Service'.

Tendering was one of the most far reaching of the changes which the London Regional Transport Act of 1984 would bring about. No longer could the red buses of LT assume they would operate all services in the London area. The 13 routes of 1985 were only the first of many and not only in the suburbs. Soon famous routes operating through the heart of the West End and the City would pass from LT operation to a variety of other companies, each providing vehicles in their own distinctive liveries.

Back in my home town the long awaited 'proper' bus station at West Croydon was opened, on the site of the existing, temporary affair. Colourful and stylish, it offered greater and more comfortable undercover waiting areas and various other facilities, including an enquiry office.

Both Routemaster and DMS fleets continued to decline. Over 300 RMs disappeared in 1985 while virtually the only DMSs still in passenger service were the B20 variation, which it had been decided to keep for a while and have overhauled. Very little of this was done at Aldenham, it being found cheaper to contract out the work. The writing was on the wall not only for Aldenham but, unthinkable as it might seem, Chiswick too.

Right:
The Green Line network opens out. TPL92 at Oxford coach station about to set off for London.

Below:
One of the massive Green Line Leyland Olympian/ECW coaches, LRC12, heads along the Embankment.

1986

Aldenham works closed on 14 November 1986. Ironically one of its last contracts was to overhaul and repaint a fleet of Routemasters for operation in Scotland. On 26 October 1986 deregulation arrived in the United Kingdom, everywhere except London that is. The consequences were extraordinary. Any route which seemed to offer even the slimmest chance of a profit was fiercely fought for. Cheap-to-run minibuses became increasingly popular, while at the same time in many towns and cities full size double-deckers competed on the busiest routes. A bus with a conductor could save precious seconds on an OPO rival, especially a bus with an open rear platform. What could be more suitable than an elderly but well looked after and reliable Routemaster? Well over 100 were bought for work in Scotland and when I visited Glasgow in October of the following year I found the Routemasters of Clydeside and Kelvin Scottish perfectly at home there, one of their favourite gathering places being beneath the handsome iron and glass screen of Central station. All were RMs except for RML900 (sold in damaged condition), and I came across it working route 38, not between Victoria station and Clapton, but from Glasgow Centre to

Johnstone adorned in a livery of red, yellow and white and the title *Oor Wullie's Special* after a famous cartoon character in the *Sunday Post*.

London's last new Mark I Metrobuses, M1439/40, were delivered in January 1986. Like their contemporaries the Titans, they have proved to be generally reliable and efficient and, although a few have been sold, the vast majority are still at work in London. Two Mark II Metrobuses, without the distinctive dropped windscreen, were delivered for evaluation trials in 1984: M1441 with a Gardner 6LXB engine and M1442 with a Cummins L10. These trials were intended to enable LT to choose its next generation of double-deckers and included the Leyland Olympians and Dennis Dominators mentioned earlier, and also three Volvo Ailsa B55s – one of which had two staircases. M1006-29 were delivered as Airbuses, linking central London with Heathrow via the M4, and were fitted with coach type seats, carpets upstairs, luggage lockers and, a little later, lifts for disabled access. The Metrobus proved very popular with provincial operators and some of these versions have subsequently appeared, secondhand, in London.

The vintage appeal of the Routemaster was recognised when 50 were put to work on the London Sightseeing Tour. Aldenham was given the £250,000

Above:
Aldenham in its heyday with a fleet of early RTLs – and one RT – waiting to take workers home to various parts of London and the Home Counties.

Left:
Clydeside's RML900 at work in Glasgow.

Above:
The former Northern General RMT2793 on sightseeing duties in the Haymarket.

contract to carry out the conversion work. 11 were RCLs, 19 were standard RMs and, most interestingly, 20 were standard RMs converted to open-toppers. The latter proved very popular and helped increase LT's share of the much fought-for sightseeing market. A fascinating addition to the open-top fleet was one of the former Northern General front-entrance Routemasters, EUP 406B. Repainted, like the others, in traditional livery with gold, underlined fleetname and numbered RMT2793, it passed officially into LT ownership in 1987. Thus, finally, 25 years after the appearance of RMF1254, a member of the class entered passenger service with LT. It was not, however, the first front-entrance RM to operate the sightseeing service in LT ownership, for six former BEA RMAs were transferred from staff bus duties at the end of 1986, fitted with RCL-type front indicators, re-upholstered and brought up to standard in various other ways, ready for the 1987 season. The sightseeing fleet, based at Battersea garage, had by now become one of the most interesting aspects of the London bus scene. Over the years various Routemasters have come and gone from the sightseeing fleet; alterations and modifications have been made, none of which – as we shall see – has lessened its appeal, with the exception of some which briefly carried a fairly hideous all-over advert for McDonalds.

As startling as open-top Routemasters was the appearance of 25-seat minibuses in traditional red livery on a central London route. Nineteen Optare City Pacers on Volkswagen chassis entered service on 25 October on new route C1 from Westminster to Kensington. Classified OV, although this didn't appear anywhere on the vehicles, with D338 JUM-D356 JUM registrations, they operated from the basement of Victoria garage. I took a ride on one during the first month of operation, and although one's initial reaction was that anything other than a full-sized double-decker was quite out of order, I rapidly changed my opinion, not only on account of the quality of the interior appointments but chiefly the quality of the drivers. Not surprisingly the general public was somewhat bemused by the sudden, virtually unpublicised appearance of such vehicles in the middle of the West End. Outside Harrods one little old lady half entered the bus and then got into a long and confused conversation with our lady driver as to just where she, the old lady, wished to go, and whether the bus went there too. Our driver was patience itself and infinitely polite, as she was with a number of other enquiries all along the route. I was much impressed. The handsome little minibuses were branded Hoppas, a snappy title which caught on and was used elsewhere beyond the capital although, truth to tell, it would have been most appropriately applied to RMs with their open rear platforms on and off of which one really could hop.

More Leyland Tiger coaches, BTL34-53 with Berkhof bodies, and TDL46-65 with a new design of Duple body, entered London Country service in 1986, along with five more of the massive Olympian double-deck coaches, all wearing a variety of liveries.

These were the last vehicles to be ordered by London Country, for on 1 September it was split into four separate companies. This in part recognised that it was somewhat of an unwieldy organisation, operating as it did around the fringes of the red bus area, but more relevant was the Conservative government's determination to press ahead with privatisation. Among other large and long established companies which were ordered to be broken up were Midland Red, Ribble, United and Crosville. The minister concerned, Nicholas Ridley, declared that keeping them intact would 'undermine the development of competition'. When one considers how the industry over the subsequent 10 years has come to be dominated by a handful of vast, new companies, one can only comment, 'Ho, ho, ho.'

The four new companies were London Country North East, with some 340 vehicles and headquarters at Hertford; London Country North West, with 310 vehicles based at Watford; London Country South East based at Dartford and owning 220 vehicles; and the largest, London Country South West, with 360 vehicles based at Reigate. Crawley works passed to a new company, Gatwick Engineering, and a new marketing company was set up for Green Line.

With production of the Ts and Ms at an end, a new standard double-decker entered service with LT in 1986. This was the Leyland Olympian. Three prototypes had appeared in 1984. Strictly speaking it would have been more accurate to refer to the Olympian as a Bristol for it was developed at the Brislington works of the former Bristol Company and the first bodies were built by Bristol's traditional partner, ECW at Lowestoft. The Olympian bore some resemblance to the Titan but had rather more symmetrical proportions. Classified L by LT, the first members of the class entered service from Plumstead garage in March, being put to work from Bexleyheath (briefly), Sidcup, New Cross, Norwood, Croydon and Streatham garages. They seated 68 passengers.

Royalty put in one of its ceremonial visits to the Underground system on 1 April 1986 when the Prince and Princess of Wales opened the Piccadilly Line extension to Heathrow's latest terminal, number four. Around the same time orders were placed with Metro-Cammell for 16 six-car trains of 1983 stock to operate on the Jubilee Line and to provide additional rolling stock, for passenger numbers on the Underground were increasing, not a little of this welcome upsurge being due to the popularity of the Capital Card.

Below:
Olympian L138 passing the Old Vic in Waterloo Road on route 1. It carries a registration originally belonging to RM838.

1987

The first of the tube trains ordered from Metro-Cammell went into service at the end of November 1987. Known as the Batch II 1983 stock, they were in all respects virtually identical to their predecessors. OPO had been the aim of LT since the Victoria Line had proved its feasibility in the late 1960s, although it was not popular with the unions, nor with some of the general public who felt safer with a guard with them in the carriage. However, as with the buses, economics determined crew reductions where possible and stock had been built so that OPO conversion could be carried out fairly simply. The first conversions were the Circle and Hammersmith

Above:
AN236, a Roe-bodied Atlantean of 1980, at High Wycombe in London Country North West livery.

and City lines in 1986; as it was intended to convert the Jubilee Line in 1988, only the first five of the new 1983 Batch II tube trains went into service with two-man crews, modifications to the earlier batch for OPO operation starting in October 1986.

One of the worst disasters to hit LT, since World War 2, occurred on the evening of 18 November 1987 when an escalator caught fire at King's Cross Underground station and 31 people died. It sent shock waves through the system, led to a universal smoking

Right:
The Hammersmith terminus of the Hammersmith & City Line on a hot July day with a train of modified D stock at the platform.

ban and a drastic rethink of staffing, communication with passengers and safety generally.

LT and London Country coach operation was at this time extending further and further beyond the traditional Green Line boundaries and London Liner's involvement with what proved to be a short-lived express service to Birmingham, brought six-wheelers back into the fleet for the first time since the demise of the prewar Renowns, four 69-seat MCW Metroliners of the type familiar on many National Express routes being bought. They were classified ML. These, like the sightseeing Routemasters, belonged to the Commercial Operations Unit, set up in January 1986 and known from October that year as London Coaches. Apart from the Routemasters, the London Coaches fleet at the beginning of 1987 consisted of 14 varied vehicles, ranging from two East Lancs coach-bodied Olympians and four modern DAF coaches, a type which would find increasing favour, to RT1530, the very last RT in LT's fleet, albeit unlicensed.

Chiswick works, now set up as Bus Engineering Ltd (BEL), had, in order to survive, to obtain works from sources other than LT and was now an agent and dealer for a number of transport manufacturers, Volkswagen and DAF diesel, for example.

If this took some getting used to, the London connection with the four new London Country companies was becoming even more diluted. London Country North East was the first to adopt a new livery – dark and light green and white window surrounds. All four companies were investing heavily in mini and midibuses, while London Country North West and London Country South West both took delivery of secondhand former Greater Manchester Atlanteans.

Left:
London United Leyland Lynx LX6
working from Hounslow garage
outside Richmond station.

Like LT they had three-piece indicators at the front but were arranged very differently. Their start was not auspicious with temporary and inadequate blinds, and some of the London Country South West vehicles even went into service on a route won from LT retaining their GMT livery. It was a state of affairs which did nothing to promote the image of deregulation. There were more and more operators appearing in the former Country Area and a mixed bunch they were, the quality of service and the vehicles varying from the excellent and up to date to the unreliable and antiquated.

London Country South East not only adopted a new name, Kentish Bus, but also a totally new livery, a rather stylish maroon and cream. In addition it began to renumber its routes, so that with the disappearance of many in the 4xx series, the break with LT was just about complete.

In the Central Area tendering was becoming more commonplace, with the various London Country companies taking over more former red routes, while other operators were also appearing, among them the long-established coach firm Grey-Green, which put former South Yorkshire Daimler Fleetlines on route 173 from Stratford to Becontree Heath. More Hoppas entered service in central London: C2 from Parliament Hill Fields to Regent Street and C3 from Chelsea Harbour to Earl's Court. C2 was operated by London Country North West with more Optare City Pacers which were owned by LT but leased to LCNW, and MBVs in traditional red livery. C3 had blue-liveried Ivecos and Sherpas. A minibus which was taking the country by storm at this time was the MCW Metrorider. Unlike some of the earlier 'Breadvans' it, along with the Optare City Pacers, was clearly designed from the outset as a PSV. Westlink, set up by London Buses in 1986 in the Kingston and Hounslow areas to bid for tendered routes, bought a considerable

number between 1987 and 1989, and still operates 33 of them as I write.

At the other end of the scale the final ECW-bodied L class Olympians entered service as yet another famous name, Eastern Coach Works of Lowestoft, went out of business at the end of January 1987. Many of the latest Ls went to Croydon garage and it was at this time that the first of a once quite unthinkable revival was seriously mooted, a new tram network for Croydon. This came in the form of a study carried out by LRT and Network SouthEast, advocating conversion of some BR electrified lines, street-running through central Croydon and a line to beleaguered New Addington, or 'Little Siberia' as this vast windswept development on top of the North Downs was known. Meantime the tram replacement 109 bus route became OPO and no longer served the Embankment, once a Mecca for tram enthusiasts but now virtually deserted due to the replacing buses, the 109's terminus becoming the more logical Trafalgar Square.

Routemasters were eagerly being snapped up and put to work all over England and Scotland. One of their earliest and most permanent new English homes was Blackpool. Decked out in a splendid version of the Corporation's prewar lined red and white livery, they took up work on the famous promenade, running alongside the trams, something RM1 had missed out in its home city by just two years. In 1987 they could be seen as far north as Perth and as far south as Southampton, and in London itself, although RMs were still being withdrawn, there were indications that they might yet have a future. There was opposition from many quarters to universal OPO in the capital and it seemed that London Buses itself was having second thoughts. Yes indeed. But not on Sundays. Many routes which continued to be operated by Routemasters Monday to Saturday went over to OPO on the Sabbath.

A bus which has become a great favourite of mine, the Leyland Lynx, replacement for the National and the very last in the long and generally highly honourable line of single-deckers produced by that once great firm, was beginning to appear in various liveries in London, although it never came anywhere approaching the numbers of its predecessors. Indeed a mere 11 wear LT red livery, the oldest being three delivered to Merthyr Tydfil in 1987 and brought back over the Severn Bridge from abroad two years later. London Buslines (Len Wright Travel) which had been in the very first batch of successful aspirants to run tendered services, taking over the 81 from Hounslow to Slough, replaced its DMSs with a batch of six yellow-painted Lynxes in 1987.

Many bus garages were closing at this time but an interesting acquisition by London Regional Transport was Victoria coach station, following the winding up of its previous owner, the NBC. Although red buses have never regularly appeared there Green Line coaches had already become a common sight.

1988

Yet more changes, as dramatic as any in LT's history, were forecast in the LRT Business Plan published in January 1988. Originally there were to have been 14-16 separate companies, but in the end there were fewer. One, Westlink/Stanwell Buses, was sold early, and another, London Forest, was disbanded in 1991, so that when the main privatisation programme came in 1994 just 10 remained to be sold. They were Centrewest, East London, Leaside, London Central, London General, London Northern, London United, Metroline, Selkent and South London. They would form the basis of separate, privatised companies, and would be in operation when privatisation arrived, which was expected to be in some two years' time. In other words LT, as it had been known since 1933, would disappear. If that doesn't warrant a new paragraph I don't know what does.

Privatisation arrived earlier than that in the former

Above:
Watford Bus DC6, a Carlyle Dartline-bodied Dennis Dart at Watford Junction.

Right:
On the Docklands Light Railway.

Country Area, London Country North East being sold to its management at the beginning of 1988. Inevitably a new livery was adopted, a not very lovely dark green and grey. A little later Kentish Bus and London Country North West went the same way, the former being bought by Proudmutual Ltd, a holding company for Northumbria. Very quickly exchanges began and vehicles previously at home on the Scottish border and Tyneside now found themselves operating in the Garden of England and vice versa. London Country North East went to Parkdale Holdings and Alan Stephenson, group chairman of East Yorkshire. It was soon split into two subsidiary concerns, based at Harlow and Hatfield. Meanwhile London Country South West adopted one of the most attractive of all the myriad new liveries appearing throughout the land, dark and light green with a red relief band.

The Docklands Light Railway, which was the nearest thing to trams seen in London since 1952, had been opened by HM the Queen on 30 July 1987, although it wasn't ready for the public to use for another month. This typified the problems this basically admirable but troubled innovative transport system was to suffer. Although set up by LT it operated as an independent concern and was to pass into the ownership of the Docklands Development Corporation in 1992, not without protest from those who felt that overall control of public transport in London was essential for the general good. For several years the DLR worked only Mondays-Fridays and not always then and buses have had to be used either as substitutes or in an ancillary capacity on countless occasions.

Despite the growing number of single-deck bus routes in central London, usually using small capacity vehicles, the pioneer Red Arrow No 500 ceased to operate in August 1987. It was replaced partly by Red Arrow 503 (not the original Waterloo-Victoria route which had vanished back in 1981) from Victoria to Paddington and the 73 which no longer ran to Hammersmith but turned south at Hyde Park Corner to terminate at Victoria. Its vanished western section was replaced by the revived 10 which ran from King's Cross to Hammersmith. Much the most interesting aspect of all this was that both the 73 and the 10 were operated by Routemasters. Truly it began to look less

Above:
Kentish Bus Park Royal-bodied Atlantean 275 in
Tunbridge Wells.

and less likely that OPO, whether single or double-deck, would become universal in the capital, whatever the provinces decided.

Routes were disappearing, reappearing, being rerouted and renumbered in and around London in a quite bewildering manner, while the companies operating them and the vehicles they provided were in a similar state of unpredictability. This wasn't necessarily a totally bad thing, for changing times – aren't they always – demanded changing public transport responses. The variety of vehicles, new and secondhand, could hardly have provided a greater contrast than the scene 30 years earlier when the RT and RF families had given London what was probably the most standardised fleet of any large city, worldwide. In modest numbers examples of both types could once again be seen operating in the LT area, the services of preserved examples being called upon from time to time to mark a route or ownership change or perhaps an anniversary, a phenomenon which both the preservation movement and operators were exploiting with growing enthusiasm.

After years of decline the Underground system saw a steady upsurge in patronage during the late 1980s. In this year 3.5 extra trains were converted from 1972

Mark I stock for the Victoria Line and a refurbishment programme was begun which has continued to the present day. One of the consequences of the terrible King's Cross fire was that in 1989 and 1990 Northern Line trains of 1972 stock were fitted with improved safety features and a public address system. Graffiti was reaching epidemic proportions at this time and LT was determined that it would not succumb as, for instance, New York had done. Various methods of removing the offending sprayed on paint were tried but these left marks on the unpainted bodywork and so experiments were begun with a return to painted stock. As one who had always thought unpainted Underground and tube trains were pretty uninspiring, I was delighted.

Two Victoria Line trains were given totally new interiors and externally the sides were painted in bands of white and blue with red ends and grey roofs. In both cases the result was excellent and it was decided that the entire Victoria Line fleet would be similarly treated. The work was done far away on the north bank of the Firth of Forth at Rosyth Royal Dockyard by Tickford Rail Ltd. Bakerloo and Northern Line 1972 stock has also been similarly refurbished, the programme continuing as I write.

Surface stock also began to undergo refurbishment and repainting. The seven units of A stock which worked the East London line were repainted in 1988-90, all with red cab ends and grey roofs and varying amounts of off-white, blue and red on the sides and doors. This was the prelude to the refurbishment of all the A and C stock.

1989

1989 was an eventful year on the Underground. Few of the trains were time expired but most were becoming dated and a programme of modernising them, inside and out, and improving safety on both the surface and tube lines began to make itself evident.

Passenger alarm facilities and public address systems were installed on the oldest, the 1959-62 tube trains, but otherwise there were no significant changes in livery or interior appointments. Withdrawal of this stock was expected to begin shortly, but only on a limited basis. Its replacement would be based on the three 1986 prototype tube trains, and an order was

Top:
Jubilee Line 1983 and refurbished Metropolitan Line A stock at Wembley Park.

Above:
Grey-Green Alexander-bodied Volvo B10M No 118 at Trafalgar Square bound for Hampstead Heath on the 24.

placed with BREL Derby for 85 trains for the Central Line. With these a new era would begin.

The first C surface stock unit working the Circle and Hammersmith and City lines, dating from 1970, to be refurbished, was dealt with at BREL Derby and went into experimental service in November 1989. At

the same time one of the 1961 A stock units, following on those already being refurbished for the East London Line, was sent to Metro-Cammell and returned in its new form for trials to determine whether any modifications would be needed before the main batch of units were dealt.

One of the highest profile examples of tendering occurred at the end of 1988 when London Buses lost the contract to operate route 24 and this was handed over to Grey-Green. The new year opened with the new dark green, pale grey and orange and white striped Alexander-bodied Volvo Citybuses already becoming a familiar sight wheeling around Trafalgar Square, heading down Whitehall and past the Houses of Parliament, successors of the many different types of red double-deckers which had worked this route.

Another remarkable arrival on the central London scene was Boro'line Maidstone, in other words Maidstone Borough Council, no less. It could be found initially operating a variety of secondhand double-deckers, later joined by some new Lynxes, on route 188 from Greenwich to Euston. Who would have

Above:
RMC1485 and a former BEA RMA of East London at Trafalgar Square on the X15.

thought that the successors of the ancient ginger-painted Crossleys, my earliest acquaintances in the Kent county town, would have had the nerve to oust London's own red double-deckers from such time-honoured haunts as Waterloo Bridge and Kingsway? The times were certainly changing.

1 April 1989 saw the various units, London United, London General, South London, etc, become limited companies, although wholly owned by London Buses Ltd. It was a big step towards privatisation. To the general public the change was generally only noticeable where special liveries were introduced. Those which attracted most attention were the East London vehicles which operated the X15, two RMs of London General and a Metrobus of London United. The latter brought out M1069 in an imaginative and most attractive version of the old London United livery as applied to its trams and trolleybuses, while RM89 and 1590 carried the red and white livery, with silver roof, of LT in the years 1933-9, virtually identical to that applied to the showbuses in the 50th anniversary year; it looked quite wonderful and might have been specially designed for them. Perhaps this said something about the vintage lines of the

Routemaster; more likely it was a reflection on the dourly unimaginative attitude to LT liveries since 1945.

The X15 was a new express rush hour route, the Beckton Express, running between Beckton and the Aldwych. It proved so popular that it was soon extended in the mornings to Oxford Circus with the return evening journeys beginning in Trafalgar Square. It was operated by six RMCs from Upton Park (U) garage, these former Green Line coaches being refurbished and painted red and gold. Immediately the route became the focus of much attention, something the East London company appreciated and fostered. The very last Routemaster, RML2760, which had spent all its career since delivery in 1968 at Upton Park, was later drafted to work it, as were former BEA front-entrance Routemasters, spruced up and restored to regular

Above:
South London Optare-bodied DAF DA1 at Trafalgar Square.

passenger service. The X15 and its parent route, the 15, were probably the most interesting in all central London, with RMLs, including 2760, standard RMs, two front-entrance RMAs and the RMCs all to be found working them. I was not a little surprised to leave Oxford Circus station a couple of weeks ago and, fighting my way through the assembled hordes of tourists of every hue, nationality and varying degrees of confusion, come upon an Upton Park RMC swinging into Regent Street sparkling in its just restored original Green Line livery. What next one wonders?

Around this time it became quite clear that the Routemaster had a future in the capital. London Coaches predicted that they would still be operating them into the next millenium while London Buses admitted that there would continue to be a need for crew-operated open-platform rear-entrance buses in central London for the forseeable future, and even talked about a possible successor to the RM. It also put out quite a silly statement to the effect that every Routemaster it withdrew was worn out and could not be put back into service. Various operators, not least London Buses itself, have disproved this on innumerable occasions since then.

We have seen how over the years the Green Line network had risen to the challenge of the ever increasing traffic demand for services to the various airports within its territory, which, of course, included Heathrow, the world's busiest, and Gatwick, which was not very far behind. In October a new company, Speedlink Airport Services Ltd headed by Nigel Gray,

former traffic manager of London & Country, was formed to operate these. Headquarters were at Crawley, while Staines garage was also taken over. 23 vehicles were transferred to Speedlink. By 1994 this number had risen dramatically to 61. Jetlink 747 and Flightline 777 have continued to sport a livery which is basically green and yellow, while the Speedlink service between Heathrow and Gatwick is operated by a fleet of coaches decked out in red, blue, white and yellow.

Mini and midibuses continued to flood into the fleets of the various operators in the London area, bringing in makes either never seen before or not for many decades. The ordering of 90 Renaults for Centrewest took one back to the earliest years of motorbuses in the capital, while the 28-seat body constructed by Wright of Ballymena, Northern Ireland, was a first, as was their Northern Irish registrations. At the other end of the scale a Celtic invasion from a different direction, which was gaining strength, was that of Alexander of Falkirk, its distinctive double-deck bodies becoming an ever more familiar sight on the streets of London. As I write they can be found on Leyland Olympians of Leaside Buses and London Central, London United's new Volvo Olympian Airbuses, and Scanias and Volvos of

Right:
London Buslines No 41, a Leyland Olympian with
Northern Counties body of 1990, Richmond bus station
with a Heathrow-bound aircraft overhead.

London Northern, while there are many single-deckers
with Alexander bodies, among the most interesting
being Selkent's distinctive 16 Dennis Lances.

The most striking looking single-decker to enter
service with LT for many years took up work in 1989
when DA1 – a DAF with Optare Delta 49-seat
bodywork – was bought for evaluation. I caught it one
afternoon in Trafalgar Square working the 109, a route
which never normally sees anything but double-
deckers. Optare, formed from the ashes of the Leeds
firm of Roe, has consistently produced the best-
looking double and single-deck bus bodies in the late
1980s and the 1990s.

The first of the new generation of Scania double-
deckers, S1-9 with Alexander bodies, arrived at
Potters Bar in July 1989 and took up work on the 263.

1990

Northern Counties, while long established, was not a
body builder traditionally associated with LT,
although it had provided bodies for the austerity Guys
immediately after the war; they were rather more
stylish than those of the various other suppliers for the
G class. These – Park Royal, Weymann, Duple and
Massey – had all fallen by the wayside over the
subsequent decades but by the end of the 1980s
Northern Counties, together with another long-
established Lancashire firm, East Lancashire, was
amongst the few surviving builders of double-deckers.
Both firms picked up sizeable contracts to supply
London & Country – which was how London Country
South West now styled itself – in 1989-91. East
Lancashire built bodies for eight Dennis Dominator
DDA1026s, Nos 602-9, and 48 Volvo B10M-50
Citybuses, Nos 610-622 and 648-684, while Northern
Counties put 21 bodies on Volvo chassis, Nos 623-43.

By this time the products of both firms were
becoming a very familiar sight in London, Grey-
Green, Kentish Bus, London Buslines, Capital
Citybus, Armchair – and London Buses – all owning
double-deck examples of one or other, sometimes
both manufacturers. The Northern Counties body of
the 1990 period was upright, restrained and rather
dignified but the East Lancs was stylish in the
extreme with sloping back upper-deck front windows,
married to a pronounced slope to the roof and dipped
side windows. It didn't appeal to everyone but it
could look very striking in a bold livery, which
London Country's two shades of green, red and black
stripes certainly was. It looked equally well in

Brighton, Hove and District colours, bringing back
memories of Tilling STs which worked in both
London and Brighton.

A notable feature of 1990 was the delivery of a first
order for 57 Dennis Darts. The first 27 had Duple
bodies, the next 30 Carlyle bodies and subsequent
years were to see more and more delivered.

The best looking Lynxes so far, half a dozen of
them, took up work in the London Country fleet in
1990. Numbered 311-16, examples can always be
found on route 289 which runs from Elmers End to
Croydon airport and Purley. It is remarkable that, 30
and more years after its demise, the pre-1939 London
airport still appears on bus indicators, but I guess that
this is because its famous control tower is a listed
building and the nearby Aerodrome Hotel also
remains. Much of the airfield is built over, part of it
being the Roundshaw Estate which FRM1 once
served, but a fair stretch of grass still survives and the
active Croydon Airport Society keeps the memory of
Croydon airport alive.

London & Country gained further former red bus
routes and its striking colours were being seen more
and more in central London. However a startling
reversal, at least for one who had known the 403 route
better than other green ones, was when London Buses
won the contract to operate it at the end of 1989, and

Croydon-based Olympians took over. I never did get used to red double-deckers parked beside the green at Warlingham. Chelsham garage, Mecca for so many spotting expeditions and where I encountered an NS on canteen duty, would soon disappear to be replaced by a superstore.

Twenty-three more Olympians arrived in the London Buses fleet in 1990. ECW being no more, these had Leyland bodies – not that these would be available much longer; the Leyland bodies were different in some respects, notably window arrangement. They had different route indicators, which were smaller, much less informative and of standard provincial design. Numbered L292-314, they bore the legend Riverside Bus and were sent to Stamford Brook garage to work the 237 from Shepherd's Bush to Sunbury. They are seen on other routes but I've only travelled on them on the 237 and then only when it has been raining, although I draw no conclusions from this about the weather in west London.

A one-time Croydon route which reached my home town no more, the 133, received 27 new Northern Counties-bodied Volvo Citybuses at the beginning of 1990. Running from its traditional City terminus at Liverpool Street, it headed southwestwards from Streatham to Tooting, which meant I could no longer catch it on my return home from the 67th Croydon cub pack meetings at the Endeavour in Melfort Road, Thornton Heath – although I hadn't actually needed

Above:
London & Country No 650, an East Lancs bodied-Volvo B10M Citybus of 1990 at Greenwich.

Above right:
L307, one of the Riverside Bus 1990 all-Leyland Olympians crosses the Grand Union Canal at Brentford.

Right:
ERM84 in Trafalgar Square.

to since 1948. The Volvos were numbered VC1-27 and took up work from Stockwell garage on 6 January 1990. A few months later they were joined by VC28-38 which were put to work on the 196, a route which did reach the Croydon area, terminating at Norwood Junction and serving the glorious Crystal Palace football ground, shades of Wright and Bright, before continuing on to Brixton where it has been known for misguided customers to get out and attempt to find a bus heading for Millwall. For a brief period at the end of 1989, after Cityrama with its blue Fleetlines suddenly gave up the routes, London & Country had operated the 196, Chelsham garage's Atlanteans providing rather more green than was

Left:
Selkent T1100 at the Croydon airport terminus of the 194. The airport buildings are in the background to the right of the bus.

Right:
Feltham No 331, rather a long way from Cricklewood but nevertheless looking perfectly at home on Crich's cobbles.

normally seen in that part of the world. With the contract passing to Stockwell, Chelsham garage finally shut up shop.

VC39 joined its brothers at Stockwell at the end of 1991, having possibly taken the long way round from Sweden. Not the least interesting aspect of the VC class is that although all of the VCs, apart from VC39, should bear G prefix registrations, many actually bear cherished ones nicked from RMs. VC3, for example, is WLT 803 and RM803, which was at that time operating out of GM garage, and was re-registered KGJ 24A.

There simply isn't space to note more than a fraction of the constant chopping and changing of routes and operators which has occurred since tendering arrived, but while passing through Croydon we must record that the 197 group of routes went green for a time, which was not so surprising as the southern terminus of Caterham was very nearly out in the country, a couple of miles inside the M25 periphery. South London's red Olympians ousted London & Country towards the end of 1989.

One of the most extraordinary episodes in the seemingly never-ending story of Routemaster variations was unveiled in 1990 when open-top ERM163 was shown to the public. This was a stretched version, the modification being carried out by Kent Engineering of Canterbury. An extra full-length bay from withdrawn RM458 was inserted in the middle of RM163, making it a five-bay 72-seater. Because of the modular construction of the Routemaster, such a sudden and drastic growth was perfectly feasible, resulting in the longest half-cab class of bus ever to run regularly in London. Nine further RMs were so treated that year and they have proved a valuable addition to the ever popular Original London Sightseeing Tour.

Few of London's once vast fleet of trams survived into preservation, principally because the preservation movement had hardly got under way by 1952, but one which did was the former prototype Feltham, MET No 331. Because of its centre door configuration it could not be converted to conduit operation when the rest of the fleet moved across the river to Telford Avenue in 1937 and it was sold to Sunderland. Ironically it was withdrawn from Sunderland service in 1952, the last year of trams in London, but its uniqueness was recognised and it was stored in various locations, eventually coming to that safe home of the British tram, Crich Museum. Even so its deteriorating state and complexity of construction gave little hope that it would run in the forseeable

future. Eventually the Gateshead Garden Festival of 1990 provided the spur and, with sponsorship from the Festival and British Steel, it returned to the northeast to work. The festival over, No 331 returned to Crich and was repainted in original MET livery. One golden October evening in 1995 I rode a Feltham for the first time in 44 years. The quality of the restoration, both inside and out, was quite breathtaking and as I sat gazing down the once so familiar length of the upper deck illuminated by brilliant shafts of the setting sun as we hummed up that Derbyshire hillside, all my notions of how advanced the Feltham had been for its time were confirmed.

In the workshops yet another amazing restoration, or rather re-creation, was in hand. The lower deck of former LCC E1 class No 1622 had been found years earlier and the car was now being put back together. The upper deck had to be built from scratch and the opportunity was taken to re-create 1622 as a rehabilitated E1r. This was an excellent notion as an original E1 already existed in the LT collection. The trucks had long since vanished but a pair of Feltham ones had been rescued from a field in Leeds. No 1622 had been wheeled out that day and, for the first time since 1952, one London tram had passed another. It was expected that restoration of 1622 would be complete in a year's time.

Below:
BL79 and a DMS at Richmond bus station.

Right:
SNB515, a former London Country National, working for Luton & District at Windsor.

Below right:
DWL8, a Wright-bodied Dennis Dart of Westlink at Kingston. The nose poking out of the bus station is a Westlink Metrorider.

1991

A sign of the times was the banning of smoking on all London buses from 14 February 1991. Long restricted to the upper deck, some companies had anticipated the effect of smoke on their paintwork by adopting a different colour scheme to downstairs – or inside as the lower deck was still sometimes known – but now society was sufficiently concerned about what nicotine was doing to the colour scheme of its lungs generally to go along with the measure. An extraordinary vehicle appeared on television screens at the beginning of 1991, advertising the ever more popular Travelcard. This started off as a DMS, changed midway to a tube carriage and finally decided it was a Network SouthEast train. Many wondered if it was the creation of a particularly ingenious computer graphic artist, but its appearance at several rallies proved that it did actually exist.

As one could write at the beginning of each new year in the 1990s, yet more mini or midi sized single-deck buses appeared on LT routes. The Dennis Dart

Left:
DR116, a Plaxton Pointer-bodied Dennis Dart of London United bearing 'Harrier' markings crosses Hammersmith Bridge.

Below:
Roe-bodied Atlantean AN251 of County Bus, formerly London Country North East, arrives at Romford from Grays.

was to prove far and away the most popular bus at this period and 1991 saw further variations on the theme. Early in the year delivery of the first 8.5m batch with Wright bodies, the DW class, was completed, to be followed by some 9m long DWLs. Wright being a Belfast firm, most of its Darts received Northern Irish JDZ registrations, which was logical enough but for all that was not what one expected to be seen fixed upon red London buses. Around this time the BL class, which had put in some 14 years' service in London, ended passenger duties in the capital, the last being replaced by Darts. However, as I write, some examples can still be seen performing as learners, while many of the others were sold and have popped up all over the United Kingdom. Many other varieties of single-decker, particularly smaller ones, could be seen operating LT contracts, sometimes for quite brief periods. A real curiosity was the Talbot Pullman, which although far

Above:
CV7 of Westlink, an Omni designed to accommodate disabled passengers and partly owned by the London Borough of Richmond, on its way to Queen Mary's Hospital, followed by a Carlyle-bodied Dart.

from being a proper grown up bus, nevertheless sported six wheels.

Out in the former Country Area London Country North West had been bought by Luton & District in October 1990 but Watford area buses bore the legend Watfordwide and later Watford Bus, which was just as well for one cannot imagine the citizens of Watford and its environs putting up with having 'Luton' emblazoned on their buses. Seven all-Leyland Olympians delivered to Watford in 1991 suggested that the single-decker was not quite all-conquering; however at the time of writing they remain the latest double-deckers in the fleet.

Awareness of the problems the disabled have in coping with public transport led in the 1980s to the development of Mobility Buses, specially adapted to carry wheelchairs. The first would seem to have been National LS454 which took up work in Stratford and Walthamstow in 1984. A number of other Nationals were adapted with lifts and clamps for the wheelchairs down to 1991, although many subsequently passed out of London Buses' ownership. Other vehicles were purpose-built for these duties.

In March 1991 the Government published *A Bus Strategy for London*, which sent shivers down many a spine in that it promised deregulation. It promised a

number of other things too: nine things altogether, many of which on the surface looked as if they ought to command universal support – 'encouraging promotion of bus services', 'safeguarding . . . concessionary travel', 'making bus priority measures more widespread and effective', for example. The trouble was that few believed any Conservative administration of the 1980s or 1990s really had a commitment to better public transport and that when it talked of offering more choice it forbore to mention that it was almost inevitably the better off who were able to exercise the greatest choice. Regular bus users are not generally to be found amongst the most affluent and there was no suggestion of a serious intent to increased funding. Much in the final chapters of this volume is concerned with the working out of these changes, although they are nowhere near yet complete.

1992

Two of London's standard double-deckers, the RM and the DMS, suffered very different fates in 1992. Although withdrawal of the Routemaster was still going on, its continued place in the scheme of things was made abundantly clear when at the beginning of the year London Buses announced 486 RMLs would be refurbished. For many months previously experimental work had been proceeding on various members of the class and on 24 February 1992 the first production refurbishment, on RML895, was unveiled to the press, although RML2360 was actually the first to be completed.

Back in the mid-1980s consideration had been given to a Routemaster replacement but the cost of such a one-off vehicle was far too high and so the refurbishment, about 20 per cent of the cost of a new vehicle, was embarked upon.

The modifications affected every part of the vehicle, mechanical, electrical and bodywork. The fitting of Cummins or Iveco engines had already taken place, producing a very different sound to that long associated with the Routemaster. Otherwise the most noticeable differences which met passengers were in the interior decor. This was a considerable improvement – many had long thought the RM inferior in this respect to the RT – with the seats retrimmed in a blue needlecord material, the sides below the windows lined to match, while the window surrounds and ceiling were white. This gave an altogether lighter feel to the bus. Among other changes heating was improved, flooring and handrails were updated and reflective numberplates were fitted.

The standard RM soldiered on and, rather like the RT in the twilight of its career in the late 1970s, found itself reappearing in ones and twos on routes from which it had been long vanished, filling the place of RMLs away being refurbished. Initially the work was carried out by TBP Holdings, a West Midlands firm, South Yorkshire Transport (SYT) based in Rotherham and the London Buses subsidiary, Leaside Buses. Later Leaside also took on the refurbishment of its Tottenham allocation of RMLs. Before 1992 was out another unexpected twist in the Routemaster story led to the repainting of 24 of the refurbished buses into a completely new livery. On 9 December it was announced that Kentish Bus had won the contract to

operate route 19, which until then had been worked by Routemasters of London General.

For the DMS, 1992 offered far fewer new horizons, at least within London Buses. The year opened with the 21-year association of the type with Merton garage coming to an end on 4 January. This left only neighbouring Sutton, Thornton Heath and Croydon still operating the DMS in regular passenger service. In March Thornton Heath's allocation was replaced by Ts, Sutton's went in April, and by midsummer only DMS2438, 2480 and 2494 were still working from TC on the 68 (their last central London route) and the 130. From October DMS2438 worked alone but managed to last out the year.

If Irish-registered buses had taken a bit of getting used to, along with refurbishing of Routemasters in Birmingham and Rotherham, what were we to make of a former Green Line route being operated by coaches with Dutch chassis and Hungarian bodies? Take it in your stride was the answer, for now anything was possible. Route 726, Dartford-Heathrow, passed to London Coaches in February and for it were bought 10 distinctive looking Ikarus-bodied DAFs, DK1-10, painted in a red, white, grey and black livery with '726 Expresslink' branding. Three months later London Coaches became the first London Buses subsidiary to be sold, its management team gaining control. It continues to be based at Wandsworth garage.

The once mighty Leyland company, now owned by Volvo, became an even less distinct shadow of its former self with the announcement of the closure of its Workington factory. The Lynx, the last all-Leyland single-decker, would cease production as would bodies for the Olympian double-decker, although chassis production would continue at the Volvo factory in Scotland. At least Leyland's last products for London were not the ignominious failures AEC's Merlins and Swifts had been: the Lynx, although never seen in great numbers in and around London,

still has its part to play, while the Olympian, now labelled Volvo, is still in production.

Despite the popularity of the midibus, and particularly the Dennis Dart, there was still a place for the full size single-decker. Westlink especially continued to demonstrate its affection for the Leyland National and in 1989-90 had added nine DAFs with Optare Delta 49-seat bodies. Now East London added 25 more to its fleet. The Delta, with its purposeful, sloping expanse of windscreen, was the best looking of the many well-proportioned single-deckers in production, and the East London vehicles were further distinguished by a striking livery of red and silver. The Leyland National, and it will be remembered that London Country once owned more of these vehicles than any other company worldwide, demonstrated it was far from finished with London Country's successors when a barely recognisable rebuilt version appeared with London & Country.

Above:
Newly delivered DK3, Ikarus CitiBus-bodied DAF of London Coaches outside its Wandsworth home.

Left:
An East Lancs Greenway of London & Country at the Brentford terminus of the 117. A London United Renault-Dodge RW is in the background.

Above:
London Central's SP19, a Daf Optare Spectra in Trafalgar Square.

Below:
Slough bus station with Leyland Nationals of, left to right, London United, Marshalls and Watford Bus.

This was the Greenway. Given a new 'green' Gardner engine and a complete body refurbishment inside and out by East Lancs in its Blackburn factory, Greenways would later appear in London Buses' red livery.

Among the ever more adventurous livery variations, notable was that applied to nine Alexander-bodied Scania double-deckers which were repainted red and white to operate a new rush hour express route, the X43 from North Finchley to London Bridge.

If the Delta was a handsome bus, what was one to say about its double-deck equivalent, the Spectra? Both proved conclusively that, even if a bus was basically a box, it didn't need to look like one. London's first DAF/Spectra, SP1, was shown to the public in September and the class took up work on route 3. As curvaceous as the Delta, the Spectra made all other designs look old-fashioned. Twenty-five were put into service in 1992-3. Surprisingly no others have appeared as yet in the capital, London Central subsequently favouring Olympians, and the infinitely smaller Wilts and Dorset fleet can boast more Spectras than London.

Garages continued to be closed and three long-established suppliers of many central London routes either gone or announced as going in 1992 were Streatham, only recently rebuilt, West Ham and Peckham.

1993

It still seemed scarcely believable but the prospect of trams reappearing on the streets of London came a little nearer at the beginning of 1993 with the appointment of a design team for the Croydon Tramlink. And the previous year trams had once again taken up regular operation in the streets of a British city for the first time since 1962 when the Manchester Metrolink had been inaugurated. So it could happen.

Early in 1993 the LT Museum closed for a £4 million refurbishment scheme. It was reopened by Michael Palin with a new mezzanine floor ingeniously squeezed in. Its home at Covent Garden might never have been an option, for the former fruit and vegetable market buildings had been threatened with demolition when the market itself had moved out to Nine Elms. That battle had been won and the continuing popularity of the whole complex of magnificent 19th century iron and glass structures is most heartening, but right from the start LT knew that, ideal though the location was, there was nothing like sufficient room to display its entire collection. The 1993 refurbishment has succeeded splendidly in creating more space while doing nothing to detract from the appeal of the building itself.

One of the best selling lines in the shop is bus models and it is remarkable how enormously popular these have become in the last few years. Some 50 years ago my friend Keith Ryde had a prewar tinplate clockwork toy bus approximating to an ST which I

coveted deeply and since the 19th century there have been many attempts to reproduce London buses, trams, trains and trolleys for the toy market. Those which still survive often have great charm – and a suitable price tag – but it was only in the 1980s that really accurate, mass-produced models appeared. There was, of course, the famous Dinky Toy STL dating from 1938; Corgi brought out a fairly accurate Routemaster in the 1960s as did Dinky Toys, the latter also in ready-to-be-assembled form, but rather surprisingly the French firm Solido was just about the earliest in the field with a near perfect replica, an O gauge 'Bus Londonien', an RT in both red and green liveries.

The real breakthrough came with EFE, whose first product was – surprise, surprise – an RT in 1:76 scale, OO gauge. I actually first saw one, and bought it, in Cardiff but such is the popularity of London prototypes that no doubt they sell equally well in the Outer Hebrides. In the December 1995 issue of *Classic Bus* its readers voted London liveries the most popular of all and, with Corgi's O gauge and Original Omnibus OO gauge models joining EFE, there is now a wonderful range of London prototypes (all right I know in some the sidelights are a millimetre too far to the left and the conductor has odd socks but I think

Below:
DMS2438, the last of its type in ordinary passenger service, at West Croydon bus station.

they're wonderful), although there's a strange dearth of trams and trolleybuses: I'd take out a second mortgage for a Feltham. The LT Museum has promoted several sets including one with an RM, a roof-box RT and a Red Arrow Leyland National which brings us neatly to the transformation of these latter vehicles – the real ones – into Greenways. Between 1992 and 1994, 42 Nationals were so treated by East Lancs. Interestingly, while other companies,

London & Country for example, seldom get their own transformed Nationals back, all of London General's started out as LT Nationals and have, with one exception, kept their original fleet numbers, merely having G put before the LS. Three seat 38 passengers, the rest 24.

It is now well over 20 years since the first Leyland Nationals appeared, and although they had their faults, they seem destined for a very long life, in whatever form. Former London ones, both red and green, can be seen at work all over the United Kingdom; one-time provincial ones have been bought for use in London, and in the suburbs and the surrounding rural areas they are as readily come by as out of town shopping centres. Slough bus station – that architectural and environmental gem – is a particularly happy hunting ground where they cheerfully pump out clouds of diesel fumes in which I swear I've seem the faint outline of John Betjeman's ghost hovering more than once. Two successors to the National appeared on central London routes in 1993. Metroline purchased 31 Dennis Lances with Northern Counties bodies and installed them in Cricklewood garage whence they operate routes 32 and 113, while London General bought 13 Volvo B10Bs, also with Northern Counties bodies, for the 88, a route which now operates between Oxford Circus – where it meets its brothers on the 113 – and Clapham Common. The 88 has been rather imaginatively branded 'The

Left:
The man from the Clapham Omnibus at Clapham Common with VN4, a Northern Counties-bodied Volvo of London General.

Below left:
It could be a scene from the 1940s. In fact it's LT165, on a day trip from the LT Collection at Covent Garden, leaving Crystal Palace and heading for Brighton on the 1994 HCVC run.

Below:
'Fancy meeting you here.' Former LT Titan T612, Merseybus 2612, heading for a familiar destination, passes one of the original London Country Park Royal-bodied Atlanteans, AN36 of 1972, now North Western 480, in the centre of Liverpool.

Above:
The Cobham Bus Museum Open Day at Apps Court with STL441, RMs, an M&D Volvo and various London single-deckers in the background.

Below:
An RML in Kentish Bus livery crossing Chelsea Bridge on route 19.

Clapham Omnibus', after that favourite touchstone of generations of politicians.

The very last DMS in ordinary passenger service, 2438, performed a ceremonial enthusiasts' run on 2 January 1993 and was finally withdrawn from Croydon garage on 20 January, thus ending 22 years of DMS operation with LT which wasn't at all bad for a type once so reviled. A total of 37 remained in stock with London Buses and they continued to pop up performing various duties. The most commonly seen were the 12 B20 trainers of London General, many adorned with bright yellow fronts and some of which are still on learner service as I write, although probably not for much longer.

With the DMS gone it was now the turn of the next semi-standard London design, the Titan, to be disposed of. As the eldest was 15 years old this was not really surprising. Although it found few buyers outside London when new, the Titan had served London well and buyers of secondhand ones were readily found. Some stayed in London but the best place to find them in a new environment was on Merseyside. Merseybus has specialised, like its predecessor Liverpool Corporation, in ancient, rather scruffy double-deckers. I write as one who was regularly bumped and rattled around the city in what appeared to be not quite completed Regents and PD series Titans in the 1960s. It therefore came as little surprise to find hordes of ex-London Titans, some not only in London livery but even still bearing East London fleetnames and logos, bumping and rattling past St George's Hall and Lime Street in the autumn of 1993. Rather more surprising was the fact that they were fighting for road space with equally large numbers of former London Country Atlanteans now owned by North Western and Liverline, London Country and LT Nationals belonging to C&M Travel, former LT DMSs and Bexleybus Olympians of Fareway, and even a red Routemaster, RM1776, belonging to Liverline – who also owned yet more former London Country Atlanteans. I even saw a couple of former London Metrobuses which must have arrived only days earlier, for selling of these had also started, but only just. Two years later some Merseybus Titans were still in red London livery. Certainly one has no need to feel cut off from the London scene in Liverpool in the 1990s, a far cry from 30 years ago when the only ex-LT vehicles were a couple of Bedford/Scammell articulated mobile canteens – although in the 1950s St Helens Corporation ran its own fleet of brand-new RTs into the city. One of these has been preserved as has one of the mobile canteens which went to Liverpool, London number 702B, JXC 2.

This brings us to the home of 702B, Cobham Bus Museum. Founded back in 1966 as the London Bus Preservation Trust, the Cobham premises were acquired in 1972, and despite several ups and downs – typical of all preservation groups – the trust now hosts a quite magnificent collection of former London vehicles, built between the 1920s and the 1950s, complementing the official LT collection. Not only does Cobham possess the only Tilling ST, one of the original LGOC Ts, and a sit-up-and-beg STL similar to the one at Covent Garden, but it has also brought together the only two surviving roof-box STLs, surely the highpoint of the standard London double-deck design of the 1930s, as well as one of the front-entrance Country Area versions, which ended its days as an open-top tree lopper. None of the later STLs are in working order although STL2093 was active in the late 1960s and early 1970s and appeared on the HCVC London to Brighton run, while restoration of STL2377 is coming along nicely.

Although the Routemaster qualified for inclusion in Cobham's collection of vintage buses, its adventures in everyday service on the streets of London were far from over. The strikingly liveried Kentish Bus examples took over route 19 from London Buses earlier in 1993 and later a second Routemaster route passed to a new operator when BTS won the route 13 contract. Twenty-two refurbished RMLs and, interestingly, one RM, were leased from London Buses Ltd and repainted, though this time the livery was simply a different shade of red. Not the least notable aspect of all this was that, for the first time for several years, crewed buses once again operated in central London on Sundays.

In 1993 the elderly Network SouthEast units which worked the deep level Waterloo and City Line (the 'Drain'), designed prewar by Bulleid were replaced by six 1992 tube sets of the same design as the new Central Line stock. The following year, as a result of government discussion, the line passed into LT ownership.

1994

A strenuous campaign against the deregulation of LT had been mounted ever since the notion had been mooted. Many were the individuals and groups who felt that, just as London overall had suffered from the abolition of the GLC, so its transport infrastructure would deteriorate without a single authority being in charge. There was, therefore, much rejoicing when the Queen's Speech at the opening of Parliament in November 1993 failed to include a bill to bring deregulation about. Privatisation would take place in 1994 and all routes would eventually be put out to tender but LT would continue to have overall responsibility for public transport in the capital and the suburbs.

More new full size single-deckers appeared with Selkent, 12 Dennis Lances with Plaxton Verde bodies in a rather fetching red and white livery – not many perhaps but at least it proved there was still a place for the big bus in London. However any new vehicle deliveries were quite overshadowed by the long predicted sale of London Buses' 4,600 strong fleet.

First to go, in September, was CentreWest to a management buy out. London General and London United followed a similar path. That extraordinary set up, Stagecoach, of the blue, red and orange stripes, which 10 years earlier had begun far away in the Highlands of Scotland, bought Selkent and East London; the Tyneside based Go Ahead bought London Central. Cowie, already familiar in London with its Grey-Green operation, added Leaside Buses and MTL Holdings acquired London Northern. MTL also owned London Suburban Bus, which was in the same group as Liverbus, and already buses might one day be seen operating in Liverpool and a day or so later appear in service in London. By the end of the year only South London remained to be sold, a rather alarming proportion of its vehicles being in a less than

satisfactory condition. Even that would go early in 1995, once it had got the spriggots rewired and the driver's uniforms pressed – to Cowie, which now owned more London buses than anyone else. Who would have thought it possible all those decades ago when Grey-Green was a coach company operating a fleet of Duple-bodied AEC Regals?

And so it had happened; the big one. Wow! No more LT or LT roundels on the side of buses after 62 years. All gone. It was all over.

Well, not really. The doomsday scenario of fleets of swooning enthusiasts confronted by Routemasters in

Below:
Titan T1101 of Bromley garage with Stagecoach Selkent branding at West Croydon.

Above:
A pair of London Central RMLs with route 12 branding in Piccadilly Circus.

Right:
South London's RM676 passing St Martin-in-the-Fields.

all over white with blue, red and orange stripes is never likely to happen, for it has been decreed that central London buses must remain predominantly – 80 per cent to be precise – red, although Ray Stenning has come up with snazzy motifs and variations: the Clapham Omnibus, the 12 and 36 branding amongst them. Ray and I go back a long way; I taught him art, briefly, back in the 1960s and he has probably done more to enliven British bus liveries than anyone else. Just how the 80 per cent rule will affect such liveries as the red and cream which South London applies to its elderly Routemasters operating out of Brixton on route 159 remains to be seen. These have become surely the best known buses in the land, for whenever a prominent politician is interviewed by the television cameras outside the Palace of Westminster there always seems to be a bright red and cream Routemaster going about its business in the background.

No doubt there will be many more changes of ownerships, yet more amalgamations and, should the national political picture change, then we may well see legislation and funding favour many more tram

schemes, Barking and North Kent for instance, and possibly for the first time ever, into the heart of the West End.

One London tradition which many see as being under threat is the double-decker. Virtually a British phenomenon – Berlin and Athens are the only other European mainland capitals I can recall where they are found, and they're rare elsewhere, certainly outside what was once the Empire – EEC legislation and a greater concern for the disabled pose problems for the future of the double-decker. The new generation of British trams, wherever they may be built, will be articulated single-deckers and there have been far fewer double-deck buses bought in relation to single-deckers, particularly small capacity ones, in the last 10 years than ever before. For all that the high capacity double-deck bus is uniquely suitable for moving large numbers of passengers about our cities, Manchester has its doubts. Edinburgh does not and in 1994 orders were still being placed by a number of the London companies. London Suburban Bus put into service 10 Volvo Olympians with elegant, very comfortable Northern Counties' Palatine II bodies, very similar to the Optare Spectra. The Liverpool connection meant that buses might well be transferred from Merseyside to the capital and vice versa. Kentish Bus and Grey-Green were others who also bought new double-deckers and, inevitably, a variety of secondhand ones appeared and disappeared with bewildering frequency. Titans were snapped up by many London companies, London Suburban Bus, Westlink and London & Country for example.

On the Underground the Metropolitan has always maintained its individuality and something of the air of a main line concern. Throughout the 1980s steam specials out of Marylebone could be seen running parallel with Metropolitan tracks and it was perhaps not surprising that steam has returned to the

Left:
Preserved Metropolitan 0-4-4T No 1.

Below left:
One of three former West Midlands Metrobuses operated by Westlink on the 411 seen in Kingston.

Below:
0-6-0Ts Nos L90 and L99 together with Bo-Bo electric locomotive *Sarah Siddons* with a steam special from Amersham to Harrow-on-the-Hill passing through Chorleywood. *Brian Morrison*

Metropolitan itself with a number of specials operating over its northern section. The Metropolitan's own 0-4-4T, No 1 is based at Quainton, just up the line from Amersham and Aylesbury, while former GWR pannier tanks which once belonged to LT have reappeared in their old haunts, along with other classes of preserved steam locomotives. A somewhat different fate befell the Epping-Ongar branch of the Central Line, the most rural section of the Underground. It eventually closed on 30 September 1994. But immediately enthusiasts announced plans eventually to reopen it as a preserved railway.

1995

1995 began with the sale of the last London bus company, South London Buses, to the Cowie Group. The price, £16.3 million, was considered a bit of a bargain, the reason being that the company had a problem with vehicle maintenance, something which caused the Traffic Commissioner concern. As Cowie also owned Grey-Green and Leaside Buses it now possessed some 1,100 London buses, making it the biggest player in the game. The acquisition of County Bus in 1996 made it yet bigger. Throughout 1995 there were further sales, amalgamations, renamings and mergers, to say nothing of a liberal wielding of the paintspray.

In the northern reaches of the former LT Country Area the inappropriately named Luton and District rechristened itself the vastly less specific 'The Shires'. It then went on to set up very much more specific local identities: 'network Watford', 'the Stevenage line', 'Luton & Dunstable', etc.

By this date one would not have expected any raised eyebrows if a consortium with its head office on Mars had bid for a London bus company, so I suppose no one should have been surprised when

Below:
Formal handover of the final train of 1992 Central Line stock at ABB Litchurch Lane works, 13 March 1995. *Brian Morrison.*

Above right:
Three low-floor Dennis Lance SLFs with Wright bodywork of CentreWest with Uxbridge Buses branding at Uxbridge.

Below right:
The Green Line network now extends as far east as Maidstone. M&D No 2195, a Plaxton-bodied Leyland Tiger delivered to Bebb of Llantwit Pardre in 1992, newly adorned in Green Line livery with the Invictaway leaping horse, stands in Armstrong Road garage, Maidstone, alongside a M&D Northern Counties-bodied Volvo B6 of 1995.

Westlink found itself owned by West Midlands Travel. Perhaps inevitably former Birmingham Metrobuses appeared working alongside their original London brothers in southwest London, although not for long as the three were soon sent to Coventry.

The London & Country garages at Croydon and Walworth joined with Kentish Bus's at Dunton Green to form LondonLinks. The livery chosen was very similar to London & Country's, while Kentish Bus decided on a vivid yellow and green for its buses outside London.

A further coming together brings our story right back to its beginnings in 1933. M&D had survived into 1995 as one of the very few large independents but in April it was sold to British Bus. It thus found itself in the same group as Kentish Bus and a joint M&D, Kentish Bus and LondonLinks administrative base was set up at Maidstone. In 1933 the formation of LT had seen M&D hand over its Dartford and Northfleet garages, the routes they operated, and 55 buses. Sixty-two years later Gravesend area rural routes passed to Kentish Bus, successor to LT. Since 1933 there had been a clear demarcation between where Green Line territory ended and the M&D express routes took over, although it was interesting that while Tunbridge Wells was exclusively M&D stage carriage territory, the express service to London belonged to Green Line. This came about because of

the transfer of the former Autocar M&D service to LT in 1934. Now M&D's Invictaway express routes between the Medway Towns and Maidstone and London became part of the Green Line network and by the end of the year practically all M&D coaches were in Green Line livery, although the Invictaway leaping horse symbol was retained, appearing alongside the Green Line branding.

Green Line might have abandoned its Eccelston Bridge home at Victoria but it had moved just a few metres southwestwards into a coach station in the Victoria Centre. From there it was now possible to take a regular Green Line service coach as far northeast as Norwich, as far north as Huntingdon and Milton Keynes, westwards to Oxford and Newbury, south to Brighton and east to its newly acquired Kentish termini. A variety of vehicles was used, all genuine coaches unlike the upmarket buses of earlier days; the now quite elderly but still comfortable Plaxton Paramount-bodied Leyland Tiger TP and TPL

class provided the backbone of the fleet, although many examples had been sold. I travelled on a Northumbria Tiger between Hexham and Corbridge on the River Tyne in May 1995 and came across another even further north in Princes Street, Edinburgh.

Former London Titans became equally well travelled. Westlink and London & Country snapped them up in some numbers, the red and cream ones branded for route 52 continued to operate for Metroline, while the acquisition of so many of the London Titans by Stagecoach meant that they began to be repainted into Stagecoach livery and posted to such far away places as Havant and Hastings on the south coast and Irvine in Scotland.

The new generation of double-deckers, curvaceous and comfortable, entered service in some numbers. Although there were no more of the pioneering Optare Spectras, Northern Counties Palatines and Alexander Royales appeared in various liveries, the most

luxurious being London United's fully air-conditioned Volvo Olympians with Royale bodies. These were airbuses and had luggage racks and wheelchair access downstairs and coach seats upstairs. They replaced many of the former Ms which were modified for ordinary service with bus type seats.

The low-floor single-decker, with the ability to kneel to enable elderly or disabled passengers and those in wheelchairs or mothers or fathers with buggies to board easily, had been a feature of 1994, many bearing striking liveries with a motif which looked rather like a zip painted around their middles. London United, CentreWest, Metroline, Leaside, County Bus and East London were already in the field. Although not all of them performed perfectly all the time, this very worthwhile concept was clearly here to stay. Four Dennis Lance SLFs with Wright Pathfinder bodies were put on the 408 by London & Country early in 1995 and 10 Scanias also with Wright bodies were delivered to Kentish Bus in November and December. I found them awaiting entry into service in M&D's headquarters garage, another example of the increasing links between the two companies.

What of the future? There is a lull for the moment in the delivery of new Underground trains, the last of the 1992 tube stock arriving in March 1995 and there is no need as yet for new surface stock. Construction is going ahead on the Jubilee Line extension.

As for the London bus, the great works which maintained it have both gone, first Aldenham and then Chiswick. The highly specialised London bus, often designed at least partly by its operator, starting way back before World War 1 with the B type and culminating with the Routemaster, is also very nearly in the past, although several hundred of the latter are still with us and some will survive in various forms into the next millenium. The standardisation which LT strove so hard to achieve from 1933 onwards, and finally achieved in the 1950s, has gone for ever and privatisation has surely ensured it will not return, certainly in the forseeable future.

Deregulation, which once seemed a racing certainty, would seem to be a dead issue. After 10 years of it outside London a Parliamentary working party has declared it a failure and recommended the setting up of a regulator. Do I hear sighs of 'Why so long?' from passengers and local authorities? At the same time evidence worldwide has shown that the diesel engine is a primary cause of pollution. Stagecoach East London has experimented with low sulphur diesel and there are other initiatives around which ought to go a long way to solving the problem. But both this and regulation opens the way for the tram – and just possibly the trolleybus. Croydon Tramlink is happening and the climate is becoming daily more favourable for other schemes. Within these pages we have recorded the demise of both the London tram, in 1952, and the trolleybus 10 years later. Ten years on I would not be the slightest bit surprised to be recording their phoenix-like restoration.

Below:
Dunton Green garage in December 1995. A pair of Peugeot-Talbot 22-seat Pullmans flank Roe-bodied Atlantean 678 and a Volvo with its London Country fleetname showing beneath the not too-well applied LondonLinks fleetname.